SELECTIONS FROM

THE SPEECH COMMUNICATION TEACHER

1986–1991

SELECTIONS FROM

THE SPEECH COMMUNICATION TEACHER

1986 – 1991

TO ACCOMPANY

THE ART OF PUBLIC SPEAKING

FOURTH EDITION

BY STEPHEN E. LUCAS

University of Wisconsin–Madison

McGRAW-HILL, INC.

*New York St. Louis San Francisco Auckland Bogotá Caracas
Lisbon London Madrid Mexico Milan Montreal
New Delhi Paris San Juan Singapore Sydney Tokyo Toronto*

SELECTIONS FROM

THE SPEECH COMMUNICATION TEACHER, 1986–1991

TO ACCOMPANY

THE ART OF PUBLIC SPEAKING

1 2 3 4 5 6 7 8 9 0 MAL MAL 9 0 9 8 7 6 5 4 3 2

ISBN 0-07-038988-8

The editor was Hilary Jackson;
the production supervisor was Leroy A. Young.
Malloy Lithographing, Inc., was printer and binder.

Preface

Published four times a year, *The Speech Communication Teacher* contains a variety of articles on teaching communication courses. In compiling this anthology, *Selections from The Speech Communication Teacher, 1986–1991,* I have selected 92 articles that will be of greatest benefit to instructors of public speaking. The articles cover a wide range of topics, including general teaching methods, speech assignments, critical thinking, organization and outlining, audience analysis, delivery, speech anxiety, diverse student populations, and testing and evaluation.

Written by classroom teachers for classroom teachers, the articles provide a wealth of practical perspectives on instructional resources, teaching strategies, and classroom exercises. I hope they will be of interest to all teachers, experienced and inexperienced alike.

I would like to thank the Speech Communication Association for permission to reprint these articles, and I would especially like to express my gratitude to the authors of the articles. It is my privilege to make their work available in conjunction with *The Art of Public Speaking*.

Stephen E. Lucas

Contents

Teaching Methods—General

Doug Brenner, "Scholastic Bowl Exercise in the Classroom" . . . 1

Jodi R. Cohen, "The Relevance of a Course in Public Speaking" . . . 2

Mark Fackler, "My First Public Speaking Class: An Oral Culture Adventure" . . . 3

Brian Hauck, "The 'People Pyramid': A Justification for Communication Studies" . . . 3

Faye D. Julian, "Journal Writing for the Speech Communication Classroom" . . . 4

Cathy Sargent Mester, "Peer Support Groups" . . . 6

Paul L. Miles, "Teacher Continuous Feedback Technique" . . . 6

Mary Mino, "Using Student Responses to Strengthen Course Objectives" . . . 8

Susan M. Ross, "A Student's 'Goal' Journal" . . . 9

John I. Sisco, "C-SPAN: Video Support for Communication Classes" . . . 9

Scott Smithson, "Utilizing a Teaching Journal to Increase Teaching Effectiveness" . . . 10

Richard E. Soller and James A. Benson, "Using Attendance Sheets as Feedback Vehicles" . . . 10

Audience Analysis and Adaptation

Sharon D. Downey, "Audience Analysis Exercise" . . . 12

Bruce C. McKinney, "Audience Analysis Exercise" . . . 13

David Neumann, "Selecting Messages: An Exercise in Audience Analysis" . . . 14

Rick Stern, "Audience Spinouts" . . . 15

Choosing Speech Topics

Susan Duffy, "Using News Magazines to Stimulate Topic Choices for Speeches" . . . 16

Lawrence W. Hugenberg and Daniel J. O'Neill, "Speaking on Critical Issue Topics in the Public Speaking Course" . . . 17

Critical Thinking

Melissa L. Beall, "Thinking About Thinking" . . . 19

Judith K. Litterst, "Observation Projects" . . . 20

Allison Schumer, "Speech Communication Via Critical Thinking—'It's in the Bag'" . . . 21

Delivery

Joan M. Gaulard, "To Read, To Memorize or To Speak" 23
Daniel D. Mills, "Tag Team Championship: Improving Delivery Skills" 24
Patricia Murray, "The Objective Game" 24
Lee Snyder, "Twenty-Five Speeches an Hour" 25

Diverse Student Populations

Fred Garbowitz, "Changing Classroom Populations Call for Increased Cultural Sensitivity" 26
Martin R. Gitterman, "Improving Performance by Maximizing Feedback for Native and Non-Native Speakers of English" 27
Harry Robie, "A Native American Speech Text for Classroom Use" 28
Charlynn Ross, "Suggestions for Teaching International Students" 28
Allison Schumer, "Helping International Students Adapt to American Communication Norms" 30

Group Discussion

Cynthia L. Bahti, "California Dreamin'" 31
Virginia B. Mayhew, "Pennies and Poems" 31
Bruce C. McKinney, "The Group Process and '12 Angry Men'" 31
Mary Mino, "Making the Basic Public Speaking Course 'Relevant': A Group Project" 33
David S. Neumann, "Small Group Membership Contract" 33
Joe Ortiz, "Group Interaction: Processes, Problems, and Consensus" 34

Interviewing

Roger L. Garrett, "Using Self-Critiquing Techniques to Teach Interviewing Skills" 36
Roger L. Garrett, "Helping Students Discover Interviewing Skills" 37

Language and Style

Sandra Hochel, "Language Awareness and Assessment" 39
Marvin D. Jensen, "Revising Speech Style" 39
Edward Lee Lamoureux, "Practicing Creative Word Choice With Dialogic Listening" 41
Richard McGrath, "The Slang Game" 42

Listening

Mary C. Forestieri, "Listening Instruction" 44
Enid Portnoy, "Activities to Promote Students' Speaking and Listening Abilities" 45

Roseanna Ross, "What Is in the Shoe Box?" 46
Valerie L. Schneider, "A Three-Step Process for Better Speaking and Listening" 47

Nonverbal Communication

Craig Johnson, "People's Court Comes to the Classroom" 49
Steven A. Rollman, "Classroom Exercises for Teaching Nonverbal Communication" 49
James A. Schnell, "Experiential Learning of Nonverbal Communication in Popular Magazine Advertising" 50

Organization and Outlining

Brenda Avadian and Marilyn Thanos, "Speechmapping: The Road Through Speech Preparation and Delivery" 51
Patricia Blom, "Using Group Activities in Basic Public Speaking" 52
Kevin James Brown, "Spidergrams": An Aid for Teaching Outlining and Organization" 53
Virginia B. Mayhew, "Outline the Pictures" 54
Mary Mino, "Structuring: An Alternate Approach for Developing Clear Organization" 55
Jim Schnell, "The Developmental Speech Sequence Model (DSSM)" 56

Persuasive Speaking

David H. Fregoe, "Informative vs. Persuasive Speaking: The Objects Game" 57
Roger L. Garrett, "The Premises of Persuasion" 58
Craig Johnson, "Nothing To Fear But Fear...Or Is There?" 59
Madlyne A. MacDonald, "The Key to Persuasion" 59
Howard N. Schreier, "Analyzing Persuasive Tactics" 61

Speech Anxiety

Joe Ayres, Theodore S. Hopf, and Jeff Ady, "Coping With Speech Anxiety" 62
Harry Langdon, "A Course on Stage Fright" 63

Speech Assignments—General

Barbara Adler, "A Speech About a 'Great American Speech,'" 65
J. Jeffrey Auer, "Creating an Extra and 'Real Life' Public Speaking Assignment" 65
Rhonda Ehrler, "Extemporizing Through Humor and Repetition" 66
C. Darrell Langley, "The Heckling Speech" 67
Randall E. Majors, "Practical Ceremonial Speaking: Three Speech Activities" 68
Charlynn Ross, "The Challenging Audience Exercise" 69
Katherine Rowan, "The Speech to Explain Difficult Ideas" 69
Allison Schumer, "Custom Comparison Speeches" 71

Speech Assignments—Impromptu Speeches

Kathleen Beauchene, ''Using Quotations as Impromptu Speech Topics'' 72
Randall Bytwerk, ''The 'Just a Minute' Impromptu Exercise'' 72
James Corey, ''International Bazaar'' 73
Diane Grainer, ''Creativity vs. 'My Speech Is About Avocados''' 74
Reed Markham, ''Power Minutes'' 74
Wilma McClarty, ''Nomination Speech: The Ideal Date'' 75
Bruce C. McKinney, ''The 'Jeopardy' of Impromptu Speaking'' 76
Ed Purdy, ''Painless Impromptu Speaking'' 77
Allison Schumer, ''Structure and Substance in a One-Minute Speech'' 77
Jeanette Wall, ''Me? Give an Impromptu Speech? No Way!'' 78
Dorothy Wilks, ''Two Birds with One Stone'' 79

Speech Assignments—Introductory/''Ice-Breaker'' Speeches

Helen Meldrum, ''Using *Vital Speeches of the Day* in the Introductory Speech Classroom'' 80
Sean Raftis, ''Brush with Greatness'' 80
Valerie L. Schneider, ''The Personal Experience Speech in Public Speaking'' 81
Scott Smithson, ''Interviewing: A Triadic Exercise'' 81
Lynne Webb, ''The Analogy Speech'' 82

Testing and Evaluation

W. Lance Haynes, ''Grading Student Speeches: An Experiential Approach'' 84
David Lapakko, ''Sanctioned 'Cheating' on Exams'' 85
Nancy Macky, ''Essential Pursuit: A Classroom Review Technique'' 86
Ellen L. Tripp, ''The Oral Quiz, or Letting Students Talk More While You Talk Less'' 86
Jeanette L. Wall, ''Applying Public Speaking Tools in Tests'' 87
Lynne Webb, ''A Student-Devised Evaluation Form'' 88

SELECTIONS FROM

THE SPEECH COMMUNICATION TEACHER

1986 – 1991

Teaching Methods—General

Scholastic Bowl Exercise In The Classroom

Goal: To reinforce learning, reward academic excellence, and make learning more enjoyable.

One exercise I use occasionally to add variety to the classroom is a "scholastic bowl" form of competition. This exercise can be used in place of regular class discussions (or as a supplement to them), or as a means of reviewing for a test. I find the exercise helpful especially when students are confronted with abstract or theoretical material which some may find "life-less." The scholastic bowl exercise can be used to review and reinforce important concepts and material, to make the process of learning more enjoyable, and to directly gain feedback about the levels of students' understanding and areas of difficulty.

Step 1: Develop the questions you consider important for the students to answer. The questions should center on important concepts and principles about which you wish to check on students' understanding or you wish to stress. Since I divide the "competition" into 1-pt. and 5-pt. rounds, I develop questions varying in difficulty. One-point questions are memory-type questions: "Which perspective stresses...?" "What is the label for...?" The more difficult questions may also feature recall questions, e.g., "List 4 of the criteria for evaluating theories," or may involve higher-level cognitive sklls, e.g., application, analysis, synthesis, evaluation: "In the following statement, which perspective is reflected...?" "Should all communication be 'interpersonal'?" "Why is this perspective incomplete or inadequate...?" You can also use true-false questions; the type and range of questions are limited only by your ingenuity and purposes.

The questions can either be put on index cards (in the fashion of game show hosts) or numbered on a regular sheet of paper with the correct answer and the question's point value

listed. I find it necessary to prepare over 50 questions for the exercise which normally takes around 40 minutes. Sometimes the groups move pretty quickly through the questions, so always prepare more than you think you'll need. Of course, you can shorten or lengthen the exercise by preparing fewer or more questions.

Step 2: Electronic equipment is unnecessary. You can use handbells, or the bells typically found on hotel desks, to allow students in a particular group to ring or "buzz" in and be recognized. Groups can also simply alternate to make the atmosphere less competitive.

Step 3: Dividing the class into two groups seems to work best, but other options may be used depending upon class size.

Read the question and award it to the student or group who rings in first. Since I have a sheet to record the correct and incorrect responses, I can credit the group and student with the responses they make. One way of stressing competition is to give the student the point(s) if they answer the question without group conferencing (within a 7 second time-limit), or to the group as a whole if conferencing took place.

Another alternative is to have each student in a group answer a question in a round-robin fashion to rule out nonparticipation. The group members may continue to answer questions until an incorrect answer is given. The missed questions may then go to the opposing group.

Another alternative is to give each group blocks of 5 to 10 questions and alternate between groups. The group with the most points at the end of the exercise wins.

Note: to encourage preparation the point-value of the question can be subtracted if the response is incorrect or incomplete.

Depending upon your grading system, you may choose to award the individuals or groups the points they earned or won, or use some other reward system. Of course, you may find that the intrinsic rewards of the exercise are sufficient. As a result of this activity students: can see information you think is especially important; can check on the accuracy of their understanding (you can provide feedback to improve their understanding); can be recognized and rewarded for being prepared; may learn from their peers and be motivated to prepare for the next scholastic bowl exercise.

Some disadvantages are that it may stress competition in a culture many people already find too competitive. Some students may feel intimidated and may not participate. As I have indicated, however, there are ways of encouraging participation and cooperation. On the whole, I find the exercise a useful pedagogical tool for accomplishing a variety of purposes.

Doug Brenner

The Relevance of a Course in Public Speaking

Goal: To encourage students to transfer the principles of public speaking to other forms of human communication.

In many high schools and institutions of higher education, all students are required to take a course in public speaking. The requirement baffles the student who cries, "But I'm not going to be a public speaker." Unfortunately for speech teachers, many students do not realize the value of a course in public speaking until the course is completed.

One of the most unrealized values of speech making is that the principles of oratory are appropriate to most communication situations. For instance, most forms of communication are organized around a central idea. Films, television shows, and letters communicate central ideas too. The talk in interviews and even bull sessions is organized around a key idea. Even the student who is baffled about the purpose of a public speaking requirement will admit to communicating almost all of the time. The speech teacher's task is to help the student transfer the principles of public speaking to situations that seem more relevant to the student. I have used the "scavenger hunt" exercise successfully to help students integrate public speaking skills into their lives.

The scavenger hunt is one exercise in a series of exercises that I call the "group challenge." Groups of three to five students compete for extra credit points to be given to the group that accumulates the most points over the semester. The group challege stimulates thought and discussion because students prepare for the competitions out of a desire to win the extra credit points. Since students remain in the same group all semester, units on small group communication can be worked into the course easily. Best of all, students enjoy the group challenges. The scavenger hunt exercise has proven instructive and enjoyable.

In the scavenger hunt, each group must identify correctly approximately twenty to thirty communication concepts outside the classroom. The list of "items," if you will, sends students into their own worlds to find instances of assumptions, organizational patterns, emotional appeals, and logical fallacies in music videos, television shows, movies, family discussions, and billboards. The first group to locate all of the items wins a designated number of points to be tallied into their score at the end of the semester. If a group turns in an imperfect list, the list is returned and the group must continue its search. In the meantime, other groups may submit their completed hunt and win the exercise.

What follows is a sample of items on the scavenger hunt list. You can adapt the list to your students' needs and interests easily. For instance, you can have students exemplify communication principles as they are found in business or the health profession.

1. Find a reward appeal to freedom in a political advertisement that is being aired presently on television. Whose advertisement is it? Quote the appeal and, in three sentences or less, explain how the quotation is a reward appeal. Note the channel that aired the advertisement, as well as the date and time of airing.
2. Find a magazine advertisement that persuades primarily through credibility. In three sentences or less, explain how the advertisement uses credibility. Supply a copy of the advertisement with your answer.
3. Locate a simile in a contemporary song. Quote the simile. Note the artist and name of the song.
4. Find a billboard within twenty miles of campus that specifically adapts to people over sixty years of age. What product is being sold on the billboard? In five sentences or less, explain how the advertisement appeals to the elderly. Note the exact location of the billboard.
5. Musicians often "go after" specific audiences by identifying with them. Name a contemporary singer that identifies with thirty to forty-five years olds. In five sentences or less, explain how his/her songs achieve identification.
6. Find an argument by analogy in an editorial in the local newspaper. Diagram the argument according to Toulmin's model of argument. Turn in a copy of the editorial with the argument underlined.
7. Find four different symbolic forms of your college on campus. List the four forms and identify their location on campus.
8. Find a book chapter that is arranged spatially. List the main headings in the chapter and supply the bibliographical reference for the book.
9. Movies often reinforce our stereotypes. Find a stereotype presently being reinforced in a popular movie that is playing at a

theatre within ten miles of campus. In five sentences or less, describe the stereotype. Note the name of the movie and the name and location of the theatre.

10. Find three assumptions in the reruns of one or more television series that audiences made at the time the shows were originally aired but do not make today. Paraphrase the assumptions and quote the dialogue that reveals the assumptions. Note the channel that aired the reruns, as well as the date and time of airing.

Jodi R. Cohen

My First Public Speaking Class: An Oral Culture Adventure

Goal: To create an oral culture in a public speaking class.

I was trained in mass communication, so when the department chair assigned me that first section of public speaking, I was, so to speak, quivering at the podium. Ethos? Logos? I was just a chapter ahead of students and perhaps a concept behind. To organize a course in which I had few clues and less than captivating interest, I settled on a plan that would allow me to tinker with the ideas of Walter Ong in a live setting.

My public speaking sections became adventures in oral culture.

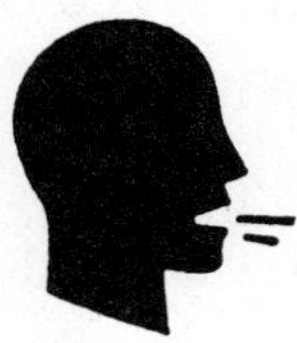

At our first meeting, and at great risk of offending the honor of the printed work, I advised the 16 students that pencil and paper were not necessary; there would be no printed syllabus; if anything I said about class structure and grading was important, we would remember it; whatever was unimportant would be forgotten—good riddance. To watch students quizzically sheath their pencils and questioningly repack their paper was, well, amusing. I was no less amazed at my own setting aside of the tools of journalism and publishing. How far could I go without a pencil?

To describe the details of organizing an orally based class without recourse to print would exceed the purposes of this space, and I should be telling you, not writing about, this adventure anyhow. But one element in the class may be an idea useful to others, even in courses where writing retains its important place: we chose one of our number to be the class "wiseperson."

Oral cultures have trouble remembering their past, I explained. Our wiseperson would remember for us. Since we had no written schedule of student speakers, the wiseperson's first task was to remember the schedule we established in class. Students who forgot would call the wiseperson for advice, guidance, and "wisdom."

Upon appointment to this noble office, a new wiseperson would do an impromptu speech urging the class to excellence and humbly accepting her/his new responsibilities. He or she would also have to teach us a campus phone number, which usually meant conjuring up a riddle or rhyme, since we could not write or otherwise record the number—"2-4-9-8, don't call till after 8" and similar diddies became our way of keeping important information intact.

Every two weeks or so, I would ask our wiseperson to secretly appoint a successor. On pass-the-mantle day, we would enjoy a short speech from our retiring sage on the nature and meaning of wisdom, the announcement of the new wiseperson, and an impromptu speech with all of its hope for the future and promises of diligence, etc. It was, of course, permitted that any wiseperson caught in a moment of forgetfulness could consult with one of his/her esteemed forebears. And if no one could remember a particular detail of scheduling or class organization, and academic chaos seemed imminent, we looked to the wiseperson to help us pick up the pieces of our oral culture and keep us marching on. Someday someone would invent paper and pencil and all would be well.

Some public address courses cannot afford to step out of the Gutenberg era as easily as we did. Writing is an essential skill. But on a campus where students can afford a two- or four-week experience in orality, the wiseperson construct held the class together. Then back to normal. Ong, after all, wrote books.

Mark Fackler

The "People Pyramid": A Justification for Communication Studies

Goal: To convince students of the potential value of their basic speech course.

Every speech instructor has looked out over the anxious opening-day faces and heard the sincere question, "Why do we have to take a speech class?" We each address that very genuine concern in our own way, trying to reduce apprehension and point our students toward an enjoyable and enriching semester. Our ability to answer that plea confidently and compassionately will, to a great extent, establish our own credibility and determine the productivity of our course.

Some of us discuss the four essential communication skills (reading, writing, listening, and speaking) and stress that, although formal education has focused on the first two, typical adults use the latter two more frequently. We justify our speech course as a belated attempt to provide instruction in the requisite skills of listening and speaking.

Others may cite the necessity of polished communication skills for current success in most careers. They also may mention the prevalence of the fear of public speaking (*The Brusking Report*, 1973) as a limitation on the success of many individuals. These approaches are useful and may be sufficient for some students.

Several years ago, while teaching speech fundamentals to high school students, I began using an argument for communication studies that my students seemed to find persuasive. Borrowing, initially, from John Irwin, Marjorie Rosenberger, and John Sloan (*Speaking Effectively*, Holt, Rinehart and Winston, 1982), I developed the "People Pyramid," a visual strategy for self-analysis of communication attitudes.

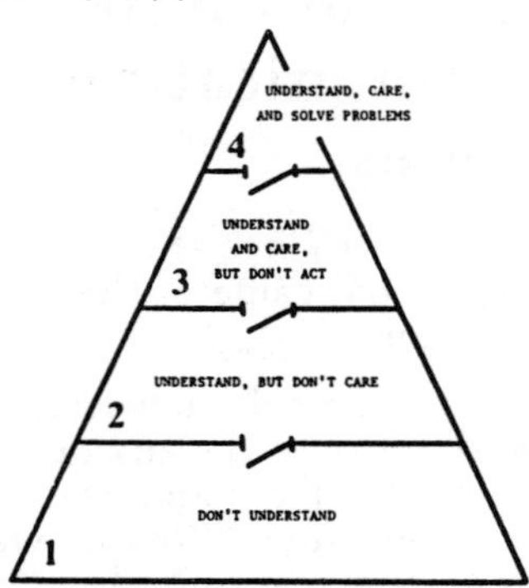

We begin with two assumptions: Everyone communicates (although not everyone communicates effectively), and everyone has a place somewhere on the "People Pyramid." We then identify at least four common categories of communicators, depending on their willingness and ability to communicate (understanding information, sending clear messages, listening and responding effectively, etc.). Students will understand quickly that they and their families, friends, and even instructors all can be located somewhere on the diagram.

Level one, the largest category, includes those people who, faced with communication situations, simply do not understand. This lack could be due to ignorance or to not yet having access to vital information. These people often are victimized by our fast-paced society, unconsciously being controlled by the information they do not understand. Each of us spends at least some of our time on this level. Students will recall times when, momentarily, they have felt helpless because they didn't comprehend.

The next level, slightly smaller, is composed of people who readily understand, but do not care. They have access to information and recognize the existence of problems, but they are apathetic. Residents of level two consciously allow their lives to be controlled by the decisions of others. Their frequent indifference makes them ineffective as communicators, although they may seem quite happy and carefree. While level one people commonly may ask, "How come?", level two people are inclined to declare, "So What!" Again, students may identify with persons in this category, recognizing that all of us occasionally spend time here.

Advancing upward to a still smaller category, we find those people who often understand and care, but do not act. They may be relatively well-informed and quite successful because they have learned to "play the game," coping with information as well as they believe they can. Often, however, they are frustrated by recognizing problems they feel unable or unwilling to solve. Each of us faces communication situations where, seemingly, "our hands are tied."

At the top of our pyramid are those few people who not only understand and care about the messages surrounding them, but also use information to solve problems for themselves and the rest of us. They are typically leaders, able and willing to use their communication skills to manage the world around them productively. Students need not be intimidated by this lofty position, for they, themselves, frequently earn respect and gratitude by ascending the "People Pyramid."

Critical questions remain for each of our students. "Where do I fit in?" We should encourage our students to analyze their daily communication efforts carefully and regularly. Although the diagram is dynamic, permitting continual movement, each of us needs to identify, honestly, the level which currently seems most representative of our attitudes.

"What do I really want to accomplish?" We should urge our students to set realistic goals for their material, emotional, and intellectual growth. Do these goals call for a two-car garage? A cabin on the lake? A college degree? An enduring family life? Service to the community?

"On which level of the 'People Pyramid' will I likely have to spend more time if I want to have a reasonable chance of achieving my goals?" Most students will agree that they will need to spend more time on higher levels, and the urgency of improved communication skills, especially speech techniques, suddenly will become clear.

"How can this speech course help me rise to those levels so I can be as successful as I'd like?" Our students now may understand how vital their basic speech course can become. If so, they will be ready to identify the specific skills that can be studied and mastered as they begin their journey toward the top of the "People Pyramid."

Brian Hauck

Journal Writing for the Speech Communication Classroom

Goal: To encourage the use and increase the value of student journals.

For years, the practice of journal writing has been emphasized, encouraged, debated, and defended by English departments; and with the impact of Writing Across the Curriculum efforts, it is not uncommon to find journals being used in classes as diverse as physics, music appreciation, and woodworking. My experience with journal writing in speech communication classes has made me a believer in journal use across our curriculum and an advocate of this multi-faceted teaching tool.

Because many students are reluctant to speak in class, it is often difficult for a teacher to know what has registered and what has not. The journal provides an excellent interactive format in which students more freely express their understanding or lack of understanding of subject matter. For instance, when I asked a class to tell me what they understood about the concept of irreversibility, I received this entry:

> I totally understand about why communication is irreversible. The easiest way to understand that sentence is to have a fight with your girlfriend.

Self revelation is the very essence of the study of intrapersonal communciation, and in studying a unit on intrapersonal, I have students write letters to themselves. Some are funny; others are self-conscious; others appear to be wishful thinking. I also have them record intralogues—internal debates in which their primitive, socialized, and conceptualizing selves articulate their arguments. Students write about the choices between study and extracurricular activities, dieting and binging, attending class or sleeping. These internal conflicts are generally written about with a great deal of imagination and a true tone of credibility.

An extremely effective way of communicating with students individually is with dialogue journals. These differ from traditional classroom journals because the teacher responds at length to students' entries rather than with brief marginal notes. This form adapts well to upper-division or graduate courses.

Journal writing in class stimulates class discussion. Starting a class period with five minutes of journal writing about the assignment and having the writing read aloud, or taking a break in the middle of class to have students transcribe their impressions, are good ways to test a variety of perceptions. This method of asking for feedback is less threatening than a pop quiz and allows contributions from the entire class.

In her book *Communicating With Myself: A Journal,* Jacquelyn Carr suggests several exercises for adding precision and clarity to language. One activity asks the writer to go through his/her journal and circle abstract, general and emotional words and replace them with more concrete, specific, and denotative terms. Labels, stereotypes, clichés, and jargon can be flagged and analyzed. Journal entries offer unlimited possibilities for the study of language use and vocabulary building.

The journal is an excellent place for brainstorming, for generating topics for research and/or papers, and for selecting individual or group projects. In preparation for symposia, I have students identify group member types (e.g., energizer, blocker, leader, procedural technician, harmonizer). One student

wrote, "Many people (in my group) wanted to be dominators. This is a negative stereotype because it causes problems for the group. Thank God we had a harmonizer." This entry suggests that she was applying her knowledge of the group's makeup. In recognizing "types," and specific typical behaviors, group members are able to function more efficiently and eliminate potential problems.

The purpose for which I first used journals in Nonverbal Communication class has expanded. I assign a field experience paper in which the students document existing theory on a given nonverbal modality (e.g., facial expression, kinesics, proxemics), and match their observations of that particular nonverbal classification with the theory. Deciding on which modality to concentrate had always been a problem. However, when looking through student journals, I realized that most students selectively observed one modality more than others. By pointing this out to the student, I am able to focus their attention on a specific form of nonverbal communication. Careful observation and recording of journal entries will identify individual selective perceptions and attitudes as well as tracing class trends and assessments of class goals.

What I find most useful and most rewarding about journal use is getting to know students in new and exciting ways. My perceptions are formed by their looks, demeanor, where they sit in class and whether or not they contribute to class discussion. I am often reminded by journal entries that my assessments may be flawed, for I often find in their writings new perspectives on students whom I thought I knew. And I am constantly alerted that the "blind pane" in my Johari window might need shrinking. I never cease to be amazed at how many strange mannerisms I have, what my dress and posture reflect about how I feel on a particular day, and what idiosyncratic behaviors I've developed. But I profit by this kind of disclosure, for if I am to ask students to trust me with their observations of themselves and their peers, it is to be expected (and appreciated) that they not be fearful of being candid about me.

Journal writing is not a new idea, but there are new applications we may find in the speech communication curriculum. A colleague has her students in the public speaking class record on the first day what they expect of the class and what they most fear. She uses those entries to structure her lecture about the goals and common anxieties of the class. She has students record their reactions to peer evaluations, and she asks students to record in journals their expectations of their own performances before a speaking assignment and their evaluations of their performances after the speeches are given. Another colleague uses journals in oral interpretation to analyze the literary merits of the works performed in her classes. And another colleague plans to use the journal as a learning tool in his speech anxiety classes. Group, interpersonal, organizational, and persuasion classes might well find a use for this journal.

Journal evaluation is not easy. It's time-consuming and often frustrating and boring, but it is worthwhile. By using focused journal writing, we have a tool for an assessment of our teaching while allowing our students to have an active and expressive voice in their learning.

Faye D. Julian

Peer Support Groups

Goal: To personalize the introductory speaking course and encourage students to share responsibility for one another's skill improvement.

Most required speech fundamentals courses create a common motivational problem for the students enrolled. The students' initial perception is that the course is a temporary thorn in the side of their calculated progress through the curriculum in their particular majors. In their youth and inexperience, students don't see a direct relevance of speaking and listening skills to their future career needs. Consequently, they resist investing much time and mental energy in the speech class assignments.

I have always found it best to combat such a negative mindset by working with students individually regarding their goals, needs, and futures. In this time of increasing class sizes, that individualization has been more and more difficult to achieve. The activity I now incorporate in my classes is one of using the class members themselves to personalize the subject matter and thus motivate one another.

The activity goes by the acronym SHARP groups, meaning Self-Help/Analysis/Review/Planning Groups. The SHARPS are peer support groups that meet on a regular, continuing basis throughout the course. Groups of 4, 5, or 6 class members are formed within the first week of the course on the basis of the students' class schedules. All the members of each group must have a common block of time free each week in order to meet together on a continuing basis with the instructor. I have found that 20-30 minutes usually is sufficient for each meeting and is about the most time five college students can find in common. The meetings are held in the instructor's office or a similar small room.

Once group membership and scheduling are established, the groups are ready to proceed. The groups first meet outside of classtime after the first round of introductory speeches. Guided by instructor generated questions, the groups consider the content and quality of one another's speeches. Discussions are fairly frank analyses of the information divulged in the introductions that give insight to the students' interests and communication strengths and weaknesses. Thus, the conversations lay the groundwork for students' subsequent speech topic and style selections.

The SHARP groups continue similar meetings between each round of speeches. In each successive meeting, the group members assume more responsibility for the questions that guide the discussion, as their sensitivity to one another and to the issues of successful communication develop and mature. Students are encouraged to be specific and positive in all of their observations and recommendations to their colleagues. Consequently, the student whose speech is being discussed learns how to polish his/her previous work and realizes the strengths upon which s/he should capitalize in the next assignment. The final session (prior to the final speeches) is particularly intensive since, by that point, the students' real ability to help each other has been demonstrated and strong camaraderie has developed in the group.

Successful use of the SHARP groups requires time commitment on the part of the instructor. The time is well worth it in terms of improvement of students' speaking skills, their appreciation of others' speaking abilities, and the resultant enhanced classroom atmosphere.

Cathy Sargent Mester

Teacher Continuous Feedback Technique

Goal: To enable the teacher to receive feedback (evaluation) of each class period with minimal intrusiveness.

This is a simple method, labelled the Teacher Continuous Feedback Technique (CFT), which makes it possible for teachers to collect student evaluations of their teaching on a continuous basis. Continuous refers to the practice of collecting student feedback after *each* class period. Teacher evaluations usually are administered at the close of the semester and serve a dual purpose: to provide administrators with information for evaluating the faculty, and to provide faculty with the students' perspective on their teaching. The value that semester evaluations hold for improving teaching is diminished for several reasons: they come too late, they lack specificity and are not descriptive, and they violate principles of learning theory due to the delay in feedback and thus, lack of effective reinforcement.

Although the comments from semester evaluations can be useful in future instruction, they provide no opportunity to respond to problems when they surface and are most relevant. It is common for teachers to read their evaluations with dismay, wishing that they had been able to address student concerns as they arose. Of course, a brave student occasionally will speak up, but most are reluctant to take the risk. When students do the teacher is faced with the dilemma of deciding whether the concern is a personal one or a perception shared by other students in the class.

End of semester evaluations contain some specific information, but general statements are more common. Such general statements provide the instructor with little concrete information to improve performance. Use of CFT not only reinforces successful teacher behavior, it also improves the instructor's ability to discriminate between successful and unsuccessful pedagogical approaches.

Administration of the technique suggested here is simple and requires no outside help. A selected number of students are requested to write an anonymous critique each meeting of the class. Diffferent students are chosen each period until all students in the class have participated. A second round then begins. The selection process can be done in a variety of ways: randon, alphabetical, volunteer. The number of students selected to participate each day probably will depend upon the size of the class. For very small classes, the system might not work as well as for larger classes because of familiarity and diminished anonymity. Using 5 or 6 students each day seems to work well in average size classes of 25 to 50 students.

At the beginning of class, a critique sheet is given to the day's evaluators. The critique sheet can be a blank piece of paper for general comments when the class previously has received directions orally. However, if specific feedback is desired, use of class time is minimized by including directions concerning the target behavior on the critique sheet.

Directions given to students can be either open-ended or specific. If the instructor is unsure of the needs to be addressed, s/he can request a general evaluation: "I would like to find out how things are going in the class. Please describe both effective and ineffective teaching that you observe during the period. Please also comment on past classes, if you like, but label comments so that they may be distinguished from today's." On the other hand, the target could be a specific concern: "Please comment on the pacing of the exercises conducted in class today. Note instances when either too much or too little time was allowed to complete the assignment."

Having respondents follow guidelines for giving and receiving feedback (C. Jung, et al., *Interpersonal Communications*, Tuxedo, N.Y.: Xicom, Inc., 1972; D. Johnson, *Reaching Out*, Englewood Cliffs, N.J.: Prentice-Hall, Inc., 1986) appears to be crucial to the successful application of this technique. Students should receive directions on at least 2 guidelines for giving feedback; being descriptive and being specific, so that the specific concern can be addressed. For example, if the student makes an evaluative statement such as "the class was boring," or a general statement such as "you get off the topic," the instructor's appropriate response is not apparent. It is much eaiser to respond to descriptive statements such as "your voice is monotone and puts me to sleep," "I would like to hear more examples," or "I have read the chapter and was looking for some application." Examples of specific statements might include such items as "I failed to see the relevance of the *Psychology Today* article," or "I get confused when you say that you will cover something later and then don't."

Being descriptive and specific applies to positive behaviors as well as to negative ones; behaviors that are reinforced are likely to occur more often. For example, statements such as "it was a great class today," or "you are a fine teacher" are non referential in behavioral terms and thus, difficult to respond to.

The number of responses received each class is small. Thus, care must be taken to analyze the responses carefully and respond appropriately. Items mentioned by more than one student are likely to be of more general concern, but there are exceptions. For example, one student might express embarrassment in response to a class exercise while others might be reluctant to do so. A list can be made of items that are of general concern, especially when they occur in successive classes, to assist the instructor's preparation for future instruction.

Guidelines for the instrutor to follow in receiving feedback (Jung, 1972) include: stating what you want feedback about, checking what you have heard, and sharing your reactions to the feedback. Application of the first of these guidelines has been addressed above.

By far, the most important of these guidelines is to share reactions with the students to the feedback. In application, this means not only changing teaching behaviors, but responding verbally (i.e. "I duplicated a copy of the overhead used yesterday for each of you because I received reports that it was too small to see;" "I received some requests to write main ideas on the board so I will be doing that more frequently.") Students will continue to respond openly if the teacher is both open and responsive to suggestions. This means that, even though some comments may seem to be unfair criticism, the teacher must handle such situations constructively (not defensively) or risk losing the trust of the student and thus, honest feedback.

Some items need clarification and class response. When doing this, it should be made clear that students need not reveal themselves as the source of the comments. Students have come to expect and comment favorably on having the critiques from the previous class period summarized. Negotiable items sometimes are voted on. One indicator of openness has been: students spontaneously (without being assigned) hand in comments on the class. Class members should be encouraged to do so.

Using the CFT appears to benefit the instructor in several areas: an increase in self-monitoring and in one's ability to discriminate between effective/ineffective behaviors; a greater sensitivity and responsiveness to students, both in and out of the class; a strengthened motivation to teach well, and an increasing ability to be open to student feedback. It will be interesting to compare the required evaluations this semester with previous semesters to check for effects that might be attributed to CFT.

Paul L. Miles

Using Student Responses to Strengthen Course Objectives

Goal: To use peer teaching to help students succeed in public speaking.

George Winger correctly asserted "The mind is a wonderful thing. It starts working the minute we are born and never stops until we are obliged to stand up and speak in public." Speech communication scholars have coined a variety of terms to describe communication-related anxiety and have recommended effective methods to reduce public speaking fears.

These fears often cause students to focus exclusively on the public speaking experience. Consequently, they fail to intellectually process the requirements and concepts necessary to excel in the course. Public speaking instructors provide students with the pertinent course information—requirements and objectives, the rhetorical situation, listening, audience analysis and adaptation, topic selection, organization, delivery, and evidence—through assignments and lectures. Instructors explain criteria for evaluating speeches and review information that will be covered on tests or quizzes. Yet, many times, students miss the point. Moreover, at the end of the semester, after all assignments are completed, students announce, "If only I knew then what I know now I would have done much better." Instructors are amazed as they recall their endless, repetitive explanations that described exactly what to do and how to do it in order to excel in their courses.

After many attempts to clearly present course information, I devised a useful way to help clarify requirements and concepts so that students better understand how to be more successful in my basic public speaking course. My guide, "Advice to Novice Speakers About How to Succeed in Public Speaking" offers suggestions from the previous semester's students who have experienced successes and failures in various aspects of public speaking. After completing all course requirements, these experienced students respond to the question, "Knowing what you know now, what would you have done in order to improve?" Students are asked to develop one to two page responses. It is explained that participation is voluntary and that the responses appearing in the guide will be anonymous and unedited. I select fifteen to twenty responses that most strongly emphasize my suggestions for excelling in the course.

The guide is distributed along with other course information at the first class meeting. Students are encouraged to study it. Because students often take their peers' version of reality much more seriously than the instructor's suggestions for success, this guide is viewed as a credible description of how to experience success and avoid failures while completing assignments. Further, it is an effective method of instructor evaluation. Each semester student responses are assessed on the basis of which concepts are regarded as most or least important. Responses are compared with my course objectives. I strengthen any weak areas through more detailed examples in my description of course requirements and concepts and by adding to, deleting from, and reorganizing the guide. Moreover, novice students have commented that this guide is extremely helpful in improving their understanding of requirements and in encouraging them to review course concepts. Students claim that they often refer to it. I was convinced of this when, during a discussion of speech organization I asked, "Why are transitions essential?" A student gave me a puzzled look, smiled, and asked, "Haven't you read the guide?"

Mary Mino

Comments from the guide:

"This course has taught me three things--to be organized, to be prepared, and to listen. Pick topics and put them together so that your audience understands you. Do good research and spend time rehearsing. Pay attention to the lectures, the comments the instructor makes about other student speeches, and most important, the comments she makes about your speech. If you do these things, public speaking is easier than you think."

"Read everything! Listen carefully! Organize! Research! Adapt to your audience! Reorganize! Practice, practice, practice! Review the comments on your speech critique sheet! Learn from your mistakes! Then, do better for the next speech!"

". . .Analyze your audience, organize the speech, plug in your research. Then make an appointment with the instructor to be sure everything is correct. If you are prepared in advance, you have time to rehearse so you are familiar with your material. If you are prepared, there is nothing to fear!"

"You can succeed in this speech communication class. Read the textbook and listen carefully during the lectures. Pick your topics with your audience in mind. Work on having clear organization and use effective supporting materials. Rehearse your speeches in advance so that when you deliver them in class you talk **with** rather than at your audience. Finally, spend time reviewing your critique sheet after each speech so you can focus on any weak spots. Most important, relax. You are given all the tools. Just use them."

A Student's "Goal" Journal

Goal: To encourage students to take responsibility for their learning in a basic speech course and to help them see personal growth as a result of their involvement.

We enroll 400 students in our basic course each semester. About two-thirds of them are required to take the course. We have found it useful to encourage our students to take responsibility for their learning in the course by using a journal to develop goals and to evaluate their own progress towards meeting those goals.

We have found this experience, introduced in about twenty minutes of class time, increases student involvement in the course. Below are the five exercises I suggest the students place in their journals.

1. Write an initial list of goals you'd like to accomplish by taking this course. (This could include things you'd like to know or be able to do by the end of the course.)

2. Write an essay explaining your choice of topic for the semester. This includes: a. Why this topic is important to me and for the audience, b. How I'll break the topic down for a sequence of informative and persuasive speeches. By requiring a single term-topic, we require students to do only one major research project. However, it is "reported upon" in three different ways.

3. Prepare a pre-speech write-up for each presentation. It should state your goals for this speech. It also should address: "What I learned from: a. Delivering my previous speech(es); b. Listening to the speeches of others — that I want to apply to this speech."

4. Prepare a post-speech write-up. It should accomplish the following tasks: a. Evaluate your progress towards meeting your goals. b. Respond critically to feedback you received on your presentation. c. Revise your initial list of goals.

5. Write a final critical analysis regarding the extent to which you've met your goals for the course. Discuss any "unanticipated positive outcomes" and make suggestions about how the course could have been more helpful to you. (I always introduce item 5 by asking students not to wait until the end of the course to make such suggestions. I say, "If NASA can make mid-course corrections miles into space, I hope I can be flexible enough to make mid-course corrections in my earth-bound communication class.")

Susan M. Ross

C-SPAN: Video Support for Communication Classes

Teachers in several disciplines and at all levels of instruction use the C-Span programming for enhancement of their courses. I am sure that many teachers of communication are well aware of this resource, but I think it worthwhile to remind all readers of the possibilities.

First, the most important dimension of the C-Span programming is that it illustrates the valuable role of oral communication in our society. The different formats for communication activity are illustrated by both positive and negative examples. The teacher of speech communication has a great resource of real world moments of public speaking, interview, group interaction, and interpersonal communication.

As you may know, the two C-Span channels, C-Span and C-Span II, are supported by the cable industry and one or the other or both are available in most locations. C-Span provides live gavel-to-gavel coverage of the U.S. House of Representatives and C-Span II provides similar coverage of the U.S. Senate. When Congress is not in session these channels carry a variety of committee hearings, interviews with politicians, reporters, and other public figures not covered at all or in full by the networks, and speeches at the National Press Club and other public forums. The network also carries sessions of the British and Canadian Parliaments. The question sessions provide the opportunity for students to evaluate how

the prime ministers communicate when under attack.

Second, C-Span allows and encourages the use of these materials for classrooms at all levels. Their liberal "permission to use" policy allows the classroom teacher to copy materials for use in the classroom. They also have seminars a couple times a year in which teachers are invited to attend sessions at their offices in Washington, D.C. to gain additional insights and uses. Their Education Director provides helpful information to those who inquire.

Third, the Purdue University Archives will sell tapes of all C-Span programming. Purdue produces an index of past programming which you might wish to make sure that your library has. While you may wish to catch a program on your own VCR, the tape can be ordered if you miss getting your machine turned on.

Finally, you will find the five minute speeches which are delivered by representatives and senators during the first hour or so of most sessions make much better examples of speeches to approximate the kinds of speeches which students give in class. If you have access to a second VCR and a limited amount of editing skill you will be able to use excerpts from the speeches to illustrate the use of various forms of evidence and organizational strategies.

All teachers should become members of "C-Span in the Classroom" to be eligible to receive a variety of helpful materials. These materials include free access to the lesson plans which accompany the various different "short subjects" Educational Series. For free enrollment write to Linda Heller, Director of Educational Series, C-Span, P.O. Box 75298, Washington, D.C. 20013. This inquiry will cause you to receive much helpful information including subscription information to "UpDate," the program guide of the C-Span channels.

John I. Sisco

Utilizing a Teaching Journal To Increase Teaching Effectiveness

Goal: To show that keeping a log of classroom experiences is a profitable venture for instructors.

As I think back to my first semesters of teaching as a graduate assistant, there were very few times when my teaching suffered because I could not recall previous teaching strategies that worked best in a particular course. However, at that time, I was teaching only one preparation per semester, with several sections, and often I taught the same course in back-to-back semesters. Now, teaching two or more different preparations each semester, and several different courses each academic year, I sometimes have difficulty recalling which exercises, lectures, examples, or readings used in previous courses were ineffective, in need of improvement, particularly useful, etc.

A solution for me has been the use of a set of "journals," one for each of the courses I teach. A basic manila folder and a few sheets of blank paper provide a good starting point for a very profitable exercise. However, notebooks, three-ring binders, or even your computer may better fit your circumstances and style.

On days that I teach, I try to find a few minutes each afternoon to conduct mini-analyses of my teaching in particular classes. Each file is labeled by class and semester for easy reference. I simply record the date and the general course subject matter, followed by a brief description of student reactions to the materials covered (lecture, exercises, or projects). Since their verbal and nonverbal reactions are fresh in my mind, this provides an important opportunity to speculate about "what worked" and "what didn't work." I often record my own general feelings about the subject matter or readings and what I liked and didn't like during that day's class session. I am always careful to include any ideas I have for improving the course in subsequent semesters. The journals provide a good record of ideas that can be better developed later, at less busy times.

My journals in a typical semester seldom are more than a few pages long, but nonetheless establish an important starting point for making beneficial changes in subsequent semesters. The journals take little time, and the rewards that come with improved teaching effectiveness are well worth the effort.

Scott Smithson

Using Attendance Sheets as Feedback Vehicles

Goal: To get feedback from students while verifying attendance.

To save time while verifying class attendance, teachers often pass around an attendance sheet, rather than call the roll aloud. Adding a question or comment at the top of the attendance sheet is a simple means of receiving feedback from students. Questions can be tailored to serve a number of relevant purposes.

Interpersonal relationships can be encouraged by asking students about themselves. For example, they can be asked to indicate what they like best about the person sitting next to them. Students can read the answers of those who sign the attendance sheet before them, or they can look at the comments on the attendance sheet at the end of the class period. Information on the sheet may serve as an ice-breaker when an individual wants to communicate with another, or it may help individuals disclose information about themselves.

Students can be encouraged to become involved in the class by asking trivia questions about current events and course material. The correct answer to the question can be disclosed at the end of the period.

Other useful purposes can be served by questions or comments on the attendance sheet. Anticipatory thinking can be encouraged, for example, by asking for ideas for possible test questions. Students can be encouraged to indicate what they like or dislike about the course. The attendance sheet questions or comments can serve to provide positive attention and reinforcement for students in the class. For example, "What is your reaction to the news that Mark received a scholarship last week?" or "Diane's speaking really improved last week. In what respect do you think it improved most?"

Here are a few suggestions if you decide to use questions or comments on the attendance sheet:

1. Start the attendance sheet at a different point each day so everyone has a chance to read comments of others.
2. Questions or comments should be simple and timely.
3. Questions should require short answers to eliminate their potential for becoming a distraction.

We have used comments and questions on attendance sheets with positive results. Each term, several students begin to express their creativity and reveal aspects of their personality via comments on the sheets. Some have mentioned it as a positive aspect of the course when they complete course evaluations. Frequently, students stop at the end of a class period to check comments of others. An interesting indicator of the sheet's appeal occurs each term: when an attendance sheet is distributed without a question or comment, the students will add one to the sheet.

Small elements of a class can contribute to the overall goals of the class. The attendance sheet, often viewed as a relatively unimportant segment of a speech class, is one such element.

Richard E. Soller and James A. Benson

Audience Analysis and Adaptation

Audience Analysis Exercise

Goal: To acquaint beginning students with the need for, difficulty of, and skills in analyzing an audience.

Effectively analyzing an audience is a skill that all beginning speakers should master. Unfortunately, it is also one of the most difficult public speaking skills to teach. Thus, I designed the following exercise to *force* students to adapt a speech topic to an audience (more specifically, to a designated and admittedly, offbeat audience) in order to exaggerate (but also to emphasize) the purpose of audience analysis.

I provide students with instruction in, and a description of, a demonstration, visual aids, or a "how to" speech assignment (which has been the most effective speech for the audience analysis exercise, although any type of speech would suffice). One week before the speeches begin, students must submit a preparation outline of the speech which includes the speech topic, general and specific purposes, thesis statement, main points, and any visual aids required.

Next, I assign each student an audience to address, based on the topics students have chosen. (The class, of course, is the audience, but should evaluate the speech from the perspective of the audience provided by the instructor.) Assigning audiences should be completed by the next class period. In selecting appropriate audiences for particular topics, the instructor should choose audiences that normally would have *no interest* in or *relevance for* that subject matter. This is what will force students to exert some effort to adjust their speeches for that audience, in order to fulfill the requirements of proper audience analysis.

The following examples may help to clarify this assignment.

Speech Topic	Audience
1. Manicuring one's nails	auto mechanics
2. Changing a bicycle tire	priests and nuns at a monthly retreat
3. How to swing a golf club	7 month pregnant women
4. Drawing pencil sketches	inner city youth gangs
5. The dynamics of hangliding	senior citizens at a weekly meeting

The point of assigning such audiences to a speech topic which the students have *already* chosen, prepared, and outlined is that they must adapt the speech to the audience and *not* vice versa, and that the speech *no longer* can be delivered in the same way because of that audience.

Once the audiences have been determined and given to each student, the teacher should instruct students of the importance and dynamics of audience analysis. Included in this lecture should be the notion that audience analysis involves making the topic and purpose of the speech significant, meaningful, personally beneficial, useful, practical, or easier for the audience. In order to fulfill these goals, the speaker must have some knowledge or reasonable "guestimation" of that audience—i.e., their size, gender, attitudes, values, interests, hobbies, knowledge of the subject, age, educational level, attitude towards subject and speaker, and so on.

Three fairly easy ways exist for adapting a speech to a particular audience. 1. Establish the *relevance* of the topic in the *introduction* and reiterate these advantages in the *conclusion* of the speech. For example, argue that knowledge of how to use a 35 mm. camera eventually might be able to help an audience of welfare recipients to learn a new trade and thereby, secure employment. 2. Adjust the *language* of the speech to fit the age, education level, or comprehension of the audience. For example, explain to a group of second graders (rather than to adult male construction workers) how to charge a battery in an automobile. 3. Use *examples* or *analogies* that fit the interests or hobbies of the respective audience. For example, explain how to make a "t-shirt dress" to an audience of truck drivers. (One student likened sewing the back and front together to attaching a truck trailer to a cab.)

After the lecture, I discuss a number of examples. Then the whole class should participate in helping their classmates figure out the best way to adapt their speeches to their audiences. By this time, students begin to get the idea and then are left to their own devices and creativity to revise their speech outlines.

This exercise has been successful every semester. It is challenging, fun, creative, and a good learning experience. The instructor exercises some creativity as well. Students seem to appreciate the instructor's good, bad, or unusual sense of humor. Normally, I assign this speech early in the semester because students tend to generalize this learning to the remainder of their speeches in the semester, evidencing mastery of audience analysis.

Sharon D. Downey

Audience Analysis Exercise

Goal: To help students complete an audience analysis exercise and identify the characteristics of poor audience analysis.

One of the concepts which my students seem to have the most trouble comprehending in my public speaking classes is audience analysis. I have tried a variety of approaches, such as having students complete audience "demographic" sheets, telling them to try to envision how to sell a product to various audiences, asking them to create a variety of thesis statements for the same speech for different audiences, and so on. Unfortunately, I still have ended up with speeches such as "How to Sustain Your Block on the Offensive Line" to an audience that is 85% female, or "Why You Should Avoid Planning a Trip to Ft. Lauderdale" to an audience the week before Spring break. I finally developed an exercise in which students see the potential disasters of poor audience analysis.

Quite by accident, I saw the videotape "Those Crazy Commercials" (Goodtimes Home Video, 401 5th Avenue, New York, NY 10016) which includes a variety of television commercials such as the blue-collar worker who claims that after 20 years his wife "finally knows how to make a sandwich"—she discovered Dow sandwich bags! My students have found these outdated commercials entertaining to view and I have used their entertainment value to teach students audience analysis.

I provide a lecture on audience analysis in which I include: (1) the importance of determining the audience's knowledge and interest with respect to the topic, (2) the attitudes of the audience toward the speaker and the topic, and (3) a consideration of the audience's needs in relation to the topic. In discussing the audience's needs, I introduce Abraham Maslow's Hierarchy of Human Needs, showing how it can help students make the topic relevant to their audience.

Next, I introduce the video with these comments: "When the folks on Madison Avenue write television commercials, they do so with a specific audience in mind—that's why you will not see a Miller Lite advertisement during the Saturday morning cartoons. I'm sure that someday, future historians might look at these commercials to discern what life was like in the 1950s and 1960s in the United States. Your task is to view the commercials from the video and try to figure out what audience they were directed to. Also, you are to think about how successful these commercials might be today." I tell them to keep these points in mind:

- What were some of the needs of people in the 50s and 60s, based on your interpretation of these commercials?
- Which commercials might work today? Why?
- Which commercials would audiences find offensive today? Why?
- How do these commercials show American attitudes have changed on topics such as sex and health since the 50s and 60s?

I have found that the comical nature of these outdated messages has been an effective demonstration of what can happen if audience analysis is ineffective. Now I am able to *show* students possible dangers inherent in poor audience analysis. After discussing the influence of the 50s videos in the 80s, I make the transition to

poor audience analysis which can produce an ineffective speech. At this time I remind students that these commercials were not necessarily examples of poor audience analysis for audiences in the 50s and 60s. As a final aspect of this exercise, I divide the class into groups and have them rewrite one of these commercials for an audience today.

If you are unable to obtain the videotape that I use, you could simply record some current television commercials.

TOP 10 TV ADS

1. PEPSI-COLA & DIET PEPSI
2. CALIFORNIA RAISINS
3. McDONALD's
4. SPUD MacKENZIE-BUD LIGHT
5. ISUZU
6. COKE
7. WENDY's
8. LEVI's
9. GRAVY TRAIN
10. STROH's Alex the Dog

Survey of 5500 viewers conducted by Video Storyboard Tests, a New York ad research firm. (*Washington Post*, Jan. 7, 1989)

After showing them to the class, ask students to perform an analysis of the target audience of the commercial. Ask questions about that audience and indicate what audiences would *not* find the message appropriate.

I have used this exercise for about 2 years and I think it has helped my students to understand and do their audience analyses for their classroom speeches.

Bruce C. McKinney

Selecting Messages: An Exercise In Audience Analysis

Goal: To have students analyze a specific audience, select a variety of pre-produced messages that suit the audience, and explain their decisions.

Perhaps one of the most interesting areas in communication deals with creating, preparing, and selecting messages directed at specific audiences. The concepts associated with audience analysis and message selection can be covered in a variety of communication courses including public speaking, persuasion, and mass communication. The following exercise should follow class information on message selection, based on audience analysis.

Prior to class, the instructor should find several magazines,

all of which are directed at different audiences. After removing a variety of advertisements, photographs, and articles from the magazines, the instructor should bring a substantial number of magazine pages to class.

At the beginning of the exercise assign students to small groups. The instructor should provide each group with a different target audience. This exercise has worked best when the target audiences are specific, such as an audience made up of white, upper-class young adults who are members of the NRA, voted Republican, are pro-choice, and have college educations. Provide each group a significantly different audience.

To begin the activity, groups should discuss their target audiences, including the collective mind-set, attitude structure, and personality variables of their audiences. Next, supply each group with a large stack of magazine materials. Instruct them to create a magazine using the materials given to them. You may want to set a page limit, depending on the time allowed. Lastly, have each group present their magazine to the rest of the class. Each group should introduce their audience, discuss the audience analysis, present the magazine title and content, and explain their choices based on their audience.

This exercise can be done in one eighty-minute period. For classes which meet for shorter periods of time, two sessions may be necessary. This exercise has received very favorable student reviews based on its hands-on nature and the way it increases students' awareness of the decisions which dictate what they see in the media.

David Neumann

Audience Spinouts

Goal: To have students develop a greater awareness of the "frame of reference" concept.

An important aspect of successful communication is a thorough awareness of one's audience and then an adaptation to that audience. However, audience analysis is one of those elements of the process of communication that many of our students do only intuitively, not consciously or intentionally.

In an attempt to have students in my communication fundamentals and public speaking classes become more aware of their own frames of reference, as well as those of the people with whom they may be communicating, I developed a very simple exercise that I have also adapted for other settings. The exercise involves a die and a set of cards with lists of possible audiences and speech topics. I have used the exercise most often with impromptu speeches.

After reviewing with the class a basic communication model, I spend a class period on frame of reference and how the frame of reference affects both what one sends and what one receives. I introduce Burke's idea of identification and the need to understand not only one's own frame and that of the other person(s) but to adapt to the other's frame of reference, to seek as much overlap in the frames as possible.

The first step in the exercise is to spend some time examining or "spinning out" the frames of reference of the class. What are their demographics? Psychographics?

They are usually more varied than the students realize. What are the issues that are important to them: world issues, vocational issues, personal issues? What makes them "tick?" The results usually suggest that (1) they have not thought thoroughly about their own frame of reference, and (2) there is more variety within their class than they anticipated. Adaptation will not be as automatic as they thought. This will be of importance when they do persuasive speeches later in the semester.

The next step is to examine their perceptions of other audiences. I choose several from the list that I have developed. Some of the categories are "divorced mother of two teen-agers, living on food stamps," "senior citizen," "empty nester," and "yuppie." There is, of course, a lot of variation within each category; realization of that is one goal of the exercise. I prepare six cards, each with different audiences, numbered 1–6; there is some overlap. For several of these audiences we go through the same set of questions as we did in examining their own frame of reference as "college students." It is interesting to hear their perceptions of the demographics of, for example, an old person. Forty and above is perceived as old. After dealing with my own depression because of *my* frame of reference, we go into the issues for that audience. What makes them happy? What makes them worry? What makes them tick? With as many questions as we can concoct for understanding that group's frame of reference, we try to detail that audience as well as possible.

If there is time during that session we go right into the exercise. If there is not sufficient time, the exercise can be used at a time later in the semester. The first step in the exercise is to roll the die. The number indicated on the die corresponds to one of six audiences.

The topic for the speech is also chosen by means of a roll of the die. The topic list consists of items I have collected. After several minutes of preparation, the speaker tries to explain the purpose and benefits of the item to the audience that was selected for them. In other words, they try to sell the item to the audience. Another possibility for a topic list includes various issues—explaining the student's position on that issue to one of the audiences. Topics include gun control, living together before marriage, drug testing, and socialized medicine. Yet another possibility is choosing one item and "selling" it to several different audiences, highlighting the various features each audience might find of value.

After the one-to-three minute speech, the class critiques the speaker's assessment of the audience, including the assumptions that seemed implicit in the presentation. The values of the exercise are (1) in making students more aware of their own frame of reference, (2) in seeing the need to be more aware of their frame of reference in order to be clearer on their own values, (3) in becoming more sensitive to the frames of reference of others, and (4) in adapting to these other audiences. I like situations in which students do the analysis and draw the conclusions. Their powers of critical thinking are sharpened and I am freed from being the person with "THE answer." This exercise seems to work toward that direction. And it is fun as well.

Sample Audience List

1. Math teacher
2. Manager of a supermarket
3. 13 year old little leaguer
4. New mother
5. Farmer
6. Foreign exchange student

Sample Topic List

1. Tea strainer
2. Seedcorn cap
3. Coat hook
4. Bar of soap
5. Pencil
6. Safety pin

Rick Stern

Choosing Speech Topics

Using News Magazines To Stimulate Topic Choices For Speeches

Goal: To encourage students to develop original speeches on SIGNIFICANT topics of current interest.

Faculty who teach public speaking for more than two semesters begin to experience feelings of *deja vu* when certain speech topics surface repeatedly. At my university, I suspect (and my students occasionally admit) that "generic" speeches appear in fraternity and sorority files. Similar speeches on anorexia nervosa, stress, bulimia, the greenhouse effect, and teenage suicide appear with unnatural frequency and little variation in evidence. Some of my colleagues prohibit certain topics. I disagree with this practice or even prescribing topics, so I set out to find a solution that would expose students to a variety of current topics that might spark their interest and structure the assignment to preclude use of file speeches or old term papers.

My solution was to require students to purchase an 18-week subscription to a national news magazine for a reduced student rate of less than $8.00, in addition to their public speaking textbook. I chose *Newsweek*, but other magazines and newspapers offer similar student discounts. Participating faculty receive study guides and worksheets on topics such as language usage, rhetoric and debate, persuasion, and developing research skills, which prove to be well-suited for supplemental exercises in the classroom.

I require student speeches to be *based* on some article or item found in the magazine. It need not be the lead article or an in-depth feature. Any article, review, essay, letter to the editor, or even advertisement can serve as the starting point. However, the student must demonstrate that something in a recent issue prompted the investigation of a specific speech topic.

This has worked well. For example, a play review of *Extremities* led one student to prepare a speech on the psychological ramifications of rape on the victim. A relatively short article on diets led another student to speak on our national obsession with thinness. Another article led to a thoughtful speech on bulimia which was unlike the stock speeches I had heard previously on the subject. Since beginning to use news magazines over a year ago, discussion during the question and answer period following each speech has improved dramatically. Articles in *Newsweek* now are cited in class discussions as often as Phil Donohue and Oprah Winfrey. Occasionally, I have questioned an opinion, or a piece of evidence, only to be chastised by my students *en masse:* "That was in *Newsweek*. Didn't you read it?" On repeated occasions, students indicate they are reading the magazine since they remember what was in articles and discuss them with considerable interest.

The second part of my solution pertains to the use of evidence in speeches. Students must use a minimum of five sources for each 6-8 minute speech. Although I am adamantly opposed to banning topics, I do

not have the same distaste for banning sources. I have found it necessary to designate some popular sources such as *People Magazine, Reader's Digest, Redbook, McCalls,* and similar sources, along with television interview shows, as unacceptable sources. *Newsweek* can only be used once in each speech. I now require students to use recent government documents whenever possible. Congressional hearings on such topics as AIDS, the homeless, automobile safety devices, orphan drugs, and so on, provide a wealth of current information from experts in a number of fields. University students generally have ready access to these documents. Small college libraries may not have these sources and the faculty member may need to substitute other reputable sources, such as *The New York Times, Washington Post, Christian Science Monitor,* or major state newspapers. I also encourage my students to use information in professional journals, and interviews with experts, whether they are city or university policemen, university administrators, campus physicians, faculty, or others on campus or in the community who are in a position to have first hand knowledge of the subject. They may not use other students as a source. The bibliography is turned in at the completion of the speech, along with any notes or material used at the lectern during the speech.

This approach has resulted in students making a concerted effort to use government documents and to seek other equally reputable sources. Their use of evidence has become more sophisticated and this, too, contributes to discussion following each speech. Increasingly, I hear student audience members ask *where* a speaker got a piece of evidence, not so much to challenge the accuracy of the evidence, but because they are genuinely interested in it. I am seeing improvement, even among weak speakers, in fielding questions. My students like to demonstrate that they have read more than the time constraints allowed them to discuss in the speech. This leads me to think that the student took a real interest in the topic investigation, probably the one element that goes the farthest in helping them give an interesting, animated speech to which they are committed. I hear fewer and fewer speeches now that sound like rehashed term papers, or worse, someone else's speech.

Using a national news weekly as the source for topics allows students to have a common base for discussion of current issues. Essentially, it gives them something to talk about together. Requiring students to use sources other than popular magazines leads initially to some disgruntlement among students, but results eventually in original speeches and animated class discussion. I have found that this two-pronged approach has made a difference in both the quality of student speeches and the discussion that follows them.

Susan Duffy

Speaking on Critical Issue Topics in the Public Speaking Course

Goal: To provide students with an opportunity to speak on the critical, contemporary issues before an educated audience.

The idea of selecting critical issues to speak on belongs to Isocrates, the Greek rhetorician and contemporary of the most famous classical rhetorician, Aristotle. He founded the most successful school of rhetoric known in the Hellenic world. Students came from all over the western world to study with this great teacher who required, above all else, that his students become well trained in speaking to the public issues of the day. He insisted that his students use broad, noble themes and not "petty" disputes.

We attempt to capture the essence of Isocrates' approach to speech training, as it has utility in the 20th century in our approach to the public speaking course at our university. We explain that all speaking in the class will be done on critical issues and we ask students to create a list of potential current, critical issue topics. We follow five steps in a Nominal Group Technique to generate a class list: 1. Silent generation of ideas in writing; 2. Round-robin recording of ideas; 3. Serial discussion for clarification; 4. Preliminary vote on item importance, and 5. Discussion of the preliminary vote.

After students have rated their choices, a typical class list of issues might include world power, drugs, toxic waste, assistance for the poor, child abuse, and terrorism. We provide students with a xeroxed list from which they select a topic area for speaking by the end of the first week of classes. Each student must prepare and deliver all his/her speeches on the same general topic throughout the course. Students may choose *only* topics on the Nominal Group Technique list.

This approach to pedagogy in the public speaking course offers specific advantages. First, students are thinking about, and preparing messages related to issues which are important in contemporary society. This enhances their ability to assess issues in future situations. The contemporary issue approach

AIDS
TERRORISM
Glasnost

focuses the student's energies on thinking *and* analysis. Historically, students in our program selected topics because of their convenience or a student's prior knowledge. Despite instructors' explanations that audience analysis should be of paramount concern in topic selection and idea development, students gave little attention to the nature of the audience for their speech. As a result of this topic-selection-by-convenience, students conducted little research on topics used for speaking assignments. The critical issue approach promotes the need for students to research historic and contemporary perspectives on their topic.

A second advantage of using this approach is that the speaker faces a relatively educated audience when delivering the speech. Traditionally, student-listeners have been "poor" audiences in the classroom because of their lack of knowledge on particular topics. By identifying general critical issues, the class focuses on a narrow range of choices. This increases the chances that one or several other students will select the same topic and become as well versed on the topic as the speaker. As a result, students prepare their speeches the way they are taught by their instructor and their textbook. They know other knowledgeable people will be part of their audiences.

A third benefit of the critical issues approach is that it permits a student to delve deeply into *a* topic and to give each assigned speech on the same topic. This provides the student an opportunity to work within that general topic to discover innovative ways of presenting information, new approaches to topics already discussed, and develop innovative solutions to problems related to that topic. This process illustrates to student-speakers that each issue is multi-faceted with multiple dimensions. It also allows students sufficient time to investigate the topic thoroughly.

Finally, the critical issues approach gives the teacher an opportunity to locate the proper balance between evaluating the content of the speech and its delivery. The techniques of identifying critical issues are applicable to a variety of speech performances *and* to students with varied interests. An important goal of the speech education process should be to develop a student's ability to identify critical issues and to discuss them in an educated manner. Isocrates suggested this type of speech training which makes the student-participant a better educated speaker *and* listener.

Our experience in using the critical issues approach in our speaking performance course is that students become more competent in preparing a speech with strong content components while attaining similar, if not improved, delivery skills. In comparison with past students, our current students become more active participants in the course during the early stages of a term, and become better educated audience members during speaking assignments in the course. They enjoy this approach because they: 1. learn something about contemporary society, and 2. rise to the challenge of being an educated orator. They begin to see the relationship between speaking skills and their society at large.

Lawrence W. Hugenberg
Daniel J. O'Neill

Critical Thinking

Thinking About Thinking

Goal: To facilitate students' transfer of thinking operations from one speech communication activity to other areas.

"How can I teach thinking? . . . My students don't know how to think. . . There's no transfer! . . . I have to keep going over the same things with these students . . ." These words are common laments from elementary through college-level teachers. The comments become shrill and filled with dismay when these same instructors learn that they are now accountable for teaching thinking because of some school- or state-mandated program.

Teaching metacognition is teaching *about* thinking. When students have metacognitive skills, they become aware of how they think, why they think, and what decisions have gone into the decision-making process. When people are proficient in metacognitive skills, they can stand back, as it were, and be objective and reflective about their thinking. In other words, metacognition is consciously reflecting on the thinking that took place (an activity we often take for granted). Metacognition makes thinkers aware of how they think and how language makes meaning for them.

Metacognition is difficult. Some experts say it is the most difficult concept and the one most crucial to the development of effective thinking skills. When presenting thinking skills workshops, this writer is often told that "I teach my students how to think and it only applies in that one activity—there's just no transfer!" Perhaps there would be more transfer (internalizing) if we were to teach our students how to stand back and reflect upon their thinking—before, during, and after each act of thinking. Flavell (1984) says there are three aspects of metacognition: planning, monitoring, and assessing. Metacognition can be likened to writing a paper or creating a research project: first one considers the problem (What problems exist? How do these problems fit my interests? How do these problems meet needs in the discipline?) and then plans how to solve the problem (How does one approach the problem? What's missing? How can an "answer" be found?). As research begins, one monitors what is happening in the process (Was this an appropriate response? If not, why not? If so, why? Where does one go from here? Now, what else do we need to know? What's the evaluation of the problem/method/solution, etc.? Is there anything else we need to know? Why? How does this all fit together?). A third aspect of metacognition is assessing the thinking (Where was the thinking clear? Where muddy? How did/should obstacles be handled? How might a similar situation be approached in the future?). When people are metacognitively effective, they (almost unconsciously) raise questions: What kinds of thinking were involved in this? What skills? What operations? How did I/we arrive at a decision? What information was discarded? What information made me/us think more? What would be done differently in another situation? Why?

Teachers typically use metacognition in planning, presenting, and assessing a lesson, unit, or course. The thinking that goes into such activities is almost second nature, so most of us don't spend a great deal of time thinking about the thinking involved. Researchers indicate, however, that the most proficient problem-solvers are very much aware of their thinking processes and are able to reflect upon what happens when they think. If we want our students to become more effective thinkers, we must teach them to *think about their thinking*. In a de-briefing session for a group problem-solving activity, a role-play, or even a discussion of speeches, we can focus on metacognition by asking students how they could have prevented certain problems and how they would approach a similar problem in the future. One way I get students to think about their thinking is to have a group of four to five students brainstorm ideas for the persuasive speech assignment. As they generate possible topics, each is to explain why s/he thinks that topic lends itself to this assignment, how it must be approached, what kinds of supporting information need to be included to make the speech persuasive, what kinds of audience analysis will help the speaker be more successful, why one approach would work and another would not, and so on. Group members are encouraged to ask questions and to explain their thought processes. Before completing the brainstorming, the group is asked to "think aloud" and discuss the thinking operations that took place individually and in the group.

When the focus is on metacognition, students and teachers will become more concerned with the process of thinking even though a product is involved or a task must be completed. When the classroom becomes process-oriented, there is more thinking and less rote memorization taking place.

Flavell, J. H. (1976). "Metacognitive Aspects of Problem Solving." In L. B. Resnick (Ed.), *The Nature of Intelligence*. Hillsdale, NJ: Erlbaum.

Melissa L. Beall

Observation Projects

Goal: To help students bridge the gaps between communication theory, research, and application.

The fact that participation enhances learning is not new or surprising. One technique that can be especially useful for developing participation-enhanced learning in many speech communication courses is the "observation project."

In the typical college classroom, learning might be described as the joining together of research, theory, and application. Typically, courses may focus on each area in varying degrees, but may not teach the student to see the connections between the areas. Students gain a "feel for research" done in an area by reading and discussing key articles and texts. Lecture material and the required textbook help them to appreciate the body of theory associated with the topic under study. If they are lucky, through examples, self awareness, or through experiences occurring simultaneously with classroom exchange, students may come to see how this material may be applied beyond the classroom.

However, do students come to appreciate how research shapes theory and how theory-building suggests research needed? Do they come to understand how sometimes tedious studies have relevance in practical applications and how common occurrences can suggest exciting research opportunities? Do they come to realize that an understanding of theory can aid in understanding human relations applications outside the classroom? Moreover, do they develop a critical thinking competence that allows them to witness an occurrence and then question how or why it occurred from numerous theoretical vantage points? Without guidance, these connections may not be made.

Instructors wishing to incorporate observation term projects into their teaching will find them to be of higher quality if they follow these quidelines:

1. *Provide students early in the term with guidance in conducting observations.*

Students have been trained to do standard library research. They often are puzzled when given free reign to people-watch. It is helpful to spend a class session discussing how to observe, pros and cons of various observation techniques, methods of collecting field notes, and the importance of the observation record. Lists of questions to ask when observing or pertinent articles on observation research may be distributed. Conducting whole-class observations of a filmed communication encounter or engaging in fishbowl exercises followed by group processing can sharpen student skills.

2. *Anticipate and discuss with students the frustration of doing this type of research.*

Sometimes students will try to take in too much at one time or will design such a microscopic study that they miss much rich information. Office conferences can allow the instructor the chance to streamline or broaden the scope of suggested projects. Try not to discourage students from projects that excite them. The football player who learns about the importance of subtle nonverbals and cohesiveness through pre-game ritual, or the aspiring politician who attends township board meetings may find the experiences very enlightening and learn a great deal from the project.

3. *Take a more nondirective approach to criticism.*

Often, you will see flaws in a student's project automatically. (Sitting in a church pew and attempting to watch nonverbal facial expressions from the congregation is difficult when you are all facing the minister!) If you see a flaw, pose some pertinent questions and let the students wrestle with the problem. Students are much more pleased with themselves and their projects when they discover and work around the limitations. They also learn how to be critical of research projects they encounter later.

Students find it useful to have key concepts, chapters in the text, or selected readings suggested at the appropriate time — what may be thought of as the "frustration point." One student, a part-time bouncer in a local drinking establishment, found Paul Keman's *Telling Lies* (1985) a particularly valuable resource for his project on detecting underage drinkers. A pre-law student, who was fascinated by legal communication styles in the office versus the courtroom, found Michael Korda's *Power: How to Get It, How to Use It* (1975) very interesting. It is wise to keep copies of exceptional projects and lists of all previously done projects. Have these available as models and idea stimulators, but be careful not to distribute them too early. Let the students be creative on their own first.

5. *Require formal progress reports to both motivate and maintain contact with students.*

Have students form hypotheses, design observation sheets of their own, investigate related literature, and summarize observation notes at least twice during the term. As a graded project, this encourages students to make headway early on and discover potential shortcomings in their own research. The instructor's feedback on these progress reports might suggest refinements or library resources plus give a student encouragement to continue. The instructor can spot students readily who are having difficulties since progress reports of those students will lack coherence and depth. These students can be invited in for a personal (yet, nonthreatening) conference. Students report that these progress checks are invaluable for keeping them on task.

6. *Have students prepare an annotated bibliography of outside readings consulted in conjunction with their own observation project.*

Encourage students to use a variety of print resources and indices. Students will discover that *good* research (not just *quick* research done to satisfy a research paper requirement) takes time and creative investigation. Students report pleasure when they find useful sources that help explain phenomena they observe. Submission of an annotated bibliography allows the instructor to assess the quality of research and places weight on the necessity for good background reading. I suggest that the instructor make note of sources that students found particularly valuable, in order to share them with students who do similar projects in the future.

7. *Provide students with guidance in organizing the written report.*

Because students are so accustomed to the standard term paper, they may be at a loss on how to organize this type of paper. Having them read selected journal articles may help them determine subheadings, but be sensitive to the fact that, for the young student, many articles are far too sophisticated. Discussing terms like literature review, hypotheses, methodology, limitations, and findings is important. Encouraging students to prepare a preliminary outline for your examination is a possible approach to take.

Judith K. Litterst

Speech Communication Via Critical Thinking—"It's In the Bag"

Goal: To develop students' critical thinking skills by providing an experiential learning task from which various communication concepts may be extracted.

This assignment, which may be used at almost any point of a Fundamentals of Speech Communication Course, emphasizes a number of communication concepts: communication process, group discussion skills, non-verbal cues, perceptions, and self-concepts. The focus may be directed by the instructor or left open-ended. What is essential is that when employing critical thinking and seeking critical thinking from one's students, the instructor: keep an open mind; be flexible; be able to evaluate arguments and the positions they support; and pay attention to the processing aspect of the task. It is also important to stay focused on the fact that right/wrong answers are not an issue but that supported, viable responses which demonstrate thinking, reflectiveness and self-awareness are.

The situation and questions in the Critical Thinking Handout should be distributed to each student. I give my students a few minutes to read the handout and ask questions for any needed clarification. Often we spend a few minutes on the word DIFFERENT in question #7. I am careful not to add too much to the structure supplied in the handout.

Question 1 through 4 are simplistic. Question 5 asks students to evaluate their previous responses (reflective thinking) and offer a rationale. Question 6 brings physical context into play as does Question 7. Question 8, like Question 5, has students again stop to evaluate their comments (reflective thinking) and offer a rationale. And it is Question 9 that is structured to have the students look back on their own thoughts, feelings, and projected actions and do reflective thinking, demonstrate self-awareness, and think critically about the communication concepts inherent in their work. It is important to stress that Question 9 asks for what has been learned from this experience not for a communication analysis of the situation.

You may choose to have your students do this as a homework assignment, or you may wish to use the questions for a group discussion. A third possibility is to have your students do the handout as a homework assignment and then discuss Question 9 in groups. This last option has the advantage of allowing the students more time to contemplate their responses. Process the activity by extracting and commenting on the communication concepts brought to light by the assignment.

I have had much success with this experiential learning activity. Although at first students usually perceive it as a "weird" assignment they become fascinated by how much they learn about themselves when faced with assessing their own thinking.

Allison Schumer

Critical Thinking Handout

SITUATION: You are walking along a street. A waist-high wall runs the length of the street on one side. You see an expensive leather travel bag in perfect condition sitting on the wall.

1. What are your THOUGHTS concerning this?
2. What are your FEELINGS concerning this?
3. What do you do?
4. Do your THOUGHTS/FEELINGS/ACTIONS all match?
5. If the answer to question #4 is no, what differs and why?
6. Where is this street you are walking on?
7. Be specific and put the street in 5 DIFFERENT locations.
8. Does what you THINK/FEEL/DO change depending on your location? Note any changes and support them.
9. What insights have you gained from this exploration:
   a. about yourself?
   b. about communication concepts?
      Be specific. Support your responses.

Delivery

To Read, To Memorize or To Speak

Goal: To provide a demonstration of the problems in translating written to oral style and to stress the value of extemporaneous delivery.

Teaching students to make oral presentations without relying on memorized or manuscript material poses a difficult problem. Seeking the reassurance of information committed to rote memory or present on the page before them, students actually complicate the task at hand. They deny the particular audience dynamic and proceed on as planned rather than attempting to respond to audience feedback. Listeners are aware that the speaker has little or no investment in them and that the same speech may be given to any group regardless of the characteristics and unique qualities which it presents.

Ability to speak from key words is not only crucial to delivering an effective public speech but also to responding to contributions in meetings (by making notes while another speaks), answering questions, and developing interview responses. Few business situations allow the luxury of scripting, and then memorizing, our response. Impromptu speaking and opinion giving are a part of everyday life. When one student asks another for an opinion on a class, teacher, movie, place, or person, no one puts off the questioner by pleading for a chance to do research, write a script, memorize it, and then return. The opinion simply is given.

Use of outlines facilitates natural delivery and audience adaptation, while providing reminders of important parts of the message. Students complain, however, that reading from a script or memorizing is easier. They express fear that they will suffer a loss for words if only a few key words appear on the page as a guide. In an effort to assure students of their existing ability to speak from an outline, I developed an in-class assignment under the guise of practice in a different skill.

Students are assigned to bring to class a short paper on the first page of which they list five steps that one may follow to find a job. These are practical, common sense steps which they think will be effective. No outside research is required and, in fact, is discouraged. On pages two and three, they devote a paragraph each to the discussion of how one may actually carry out that step.

"Ability to speak from key words is not only crucial to delivering an effective public speech but also to responding to contributions in meetings (by making notes while another speaks), answering questions, and developing interview responses."

At the beginning of class, I collect papers and fold back the cover page. I then assign students to groups of six to seven members and distribute papers so that no one has a paper written by another person in that group. This way students neither work from their own papers, nor recognize their own work.

Using the goal of comparison of what others identify as the beginning of the job search, I ask that students turn past the list of steps to page two and that each member merely read the authors' first step to other group members. No eye contact or interpretation is required. When all members in all groups have completed the first step, we discuss how it felt to listen. The overwhelming response is "boring," so we then move to the next trial.

Students now read step two aloud, but they must maintain eye contact with all other members at least half of the time that they read. In addition, the reader must "sell" the message of step two by changing volume, pitch, rate, and tone. I caution students to remain true to the author's words and not change that copy.

This round generally encourages greater discussion. While less boring for listeners, successful execution requires far greater effort from readers who often complain of losing their place and stumbling over unfamiliar words. Also, the wording does not "sound right" because of its formality.

Finally, I ask that students turn back to the list of steps and describe how to carry out steps three and four in their own words. I remind them to establish and maintain eye contact and to use conversational language. Since students are likely to remark on the similarity of steps described, description of how to carry out these steps should not pose a problem.

When students complete this last trial, we compare the three rounds in terms of interestingness to listener, difficulty for speaker, and overall effectiveness. Without exception, students choose the third trial as superior because they felt a stronger connection to one another. In addition, they were given the chance to present the information in the language and manner which they felt would be best to reach other members. Also, one could "sound like myself" rather than like the writer..

Students identified the second trial as the most difficult because it required the most effort from the speaker. It is here that I question, "Why do that to yourself?" Why devote time to the additional stage of scripting and then attempting to memorize material when use of key phrases has just been shown to be far more effective? This exercise serves as a clear reminder of the problems of manuscripting and memorizing. I refer to it throughout the term to encourage students to develop the skill of speaking from outlines.

Joan M. Gaulard

Tag Team Championship: Improving Delivery Skills

Goal: To increase speaker enthusiasm and energetic delivery through a group speaking project.

One of the most challenging tasks facing an instructor in a public speaking class involves getting students to open up and use a little energy in their delivery of a speech.

One method I have used is an activity I refer to as "The Tag Team Championships." The activity is not graded. The sole purpose of the "Tag Team Championship" is for students to realize the effect an energetic delivery can have on a speech.

This activity is designed to show students the full realm of possibilities available to them in delivery skills (i.e., gestures, body posture, vocal variety, eye contact).

Divide the class into equal-sized groups. An even number of groups will work the best for the "playoffs." Each group is then told to prepare a speech on any topic which comes to mind (time length of the speech to be determined by the instructor; 3 to 5 minutes seems to work well). Sources may also be created "out of thin air," as the focus is on energetic delivery rather than effective data gathering.

(Photo courtesy of George Mason Univ.)

Each group is to prepare a speech which includes an introduction, main points, and conclusion.

Once each group has prepared a speech, the students are to "divide" the speech up among themselves. One may deliver the introduction, another the first main point, another the second, etc.

After the speech has been divided up, the instructor tells the students that two groups will go to the front of the room and present their speech *at the same time.*

The instructor tells the students that "the goal is to keep the attention of the audience (the remaining students) focused on your group's speech. Any tactic may be used to keep attention on your group. Increased volume, odd or interesting sounds, wild gestures, jumping up and down, and anything else that you can think of is considered 'fair game'." (The instructor may wish to place taboos on certain gestures and on certain physical activities, i.e., jumping up on desks.)

Students are encouraged to keep the speech flowing by "tagging in" the person who delivers the next part of the speech (similar to professional tag-team wrestling). If possible, you may wish to take the class outside for this activity, as it has the potential to get quite loud in the classroom.

After the two groups in the front of the class have finished, the audience votes on which group best kept their attention.

Two new groups then go to the front of the room and the "competition" continues until each group has presented. After all groups have competed, the winners face off in front of the class until the "tag-team champions" are crowned.

A discussion follows the competition with emphasis placed on how an energetic delivery can enhance an individual's presence before an audience.

While not all the techniques used by the groups would be effective for many speaking situations, the students should realize two important items: 1) an energetic delivery can add to presentation effectiveness, and 2) they are all capable of putting a little "energy" into their delivery. Students also receive an added benefit in that parts of a speech (intro, main points, conclusion) are reinforced through the activity.

Daniel D. Mills

The Objective Game

Goal: To improve delivery through vocal and emotional expression.

As a teacher of public speaking, I encourage my students to speak with passion; to use their voices to arouse thoughts and feelings in listeners in order to accomplish their goals. This ability is of utmost importance in manuscript readings and in the persuasive speech. Many students can construct a well-written speech but are incapable of delivering it with clearly defined intentions behind the words they speak.

This game is a fun way to expose students to the power of effective delivery and to let them see and hear how vocal and emotional expression can enhance a speech and produce the desired effect upon an audience.

Write verbs in the infinitive verb form and put slips of paper into a hat. The best verbs are those that are "active" and can be easily expressed. Good examples are: to tease, to plead, to seduce, to whine, to cower, to swoon, to frighten, to wonder, to accuse, to inquire, to challenge, and so forth.

Next, the instructor provides a "script." Every student uses the same script to express the selected verb. I have found the first four lines of "Mary Had a Little Lamb" work well. (Mary had a little lamb, its fleece was white as snow, and everywhere that Mary went, the lamb was sure to go.) Most students will already know the lines, and their simplicity puts the focus on *how* they are expressed, rather than on the words themselves.

A student draws a verb out of the hat and must say the "script" in such a way that the audience will be able to guess the verb being played. Synonyms count—"to scare" is the same as "to frighten."

It should be noted that this exercise is nonevaluative in nature. By playing this game, students are able to see and hear how effective speakers can be when their voices, body, and emotions work together to communicate and achieve a specific goal.

Patricia Murray

Twenty-Five Speeches An Hour

Goal: To increase the critical feedback student speakers receive, encourage adaptation and ensure oral practice.

I've long felt that many students were not benefiting from their basic public speaking course as much as they could. They simply didn't practice their speeches before coming to class. Also, they didn't have an opportunity to deliver their speeches a second time so they could work on problems that were pointed out to them. Our students make 5 speeches a semester, so not enough time exists for them to deliver the same speech twice in class, which might have solved the problem.

"They simply didn't practice their speeches before coming to class."

This is the solution that works for me. First, I assign all of the students to give their 6-minute persuasive speeches on the same day. Of course, they wonder how they all will be able to speak in one class period, but the curiosity helps build anticipation. On the assigned day, I put students into groups of 4 or 5 and lead them to unoccupied sites nearby. These sites may include the lawn (in good weather), vacant classrooms, and even empty hallways. Each group is instructed to let each member give his/her speech in turn (standing up, just as in class) while the other members write critiques and give them to the speaker. (The critique sheets are simple: "What did the speaker do well?" and "How could the speaker improve most?") While the groups practice, I travel from group to group answering questions and, perhaps, staying long enough to listen to a speech.

This exercise works well during the middle or latter half of the semester because by then the students have had enough experience listening to be able to criticize their classmates constructively. During the next 3 class periods one-third of the students speak each day which is the performance pattern we use for other speeches. The difference is that, this time, I know that each of them has practiced at least once and has learned how a particular speech can be presented in a better way.

Lee Snyder

Diverse Student Populations

Changing Classroom Populations Call For Increased Cultural Sensitivity

Goal: To assist teachers in demonstrating their sensitivity to the variety of ethnic, racial, social and cultural backgrounds of students.

"Lettuce Bush," the teacher called.

"Lettuce Bush," still no response. The first day of school is usually a bit hectic and somewhat frustrating and the teacher was getting annoyed.

"Is there a Lettuce Bush here?" The teacher wanted the roll call to go smoothly and quickly because of all the first day introductory business that had to be completed. "That's Latice Bushe," a female voice said, thinly disguising her indignation.

Scenes like this one are repeated throughout the nation's schools. Being sensitive to the feelings of our students is such an important basic element in the process of effective teaching that it is unfortunate that we don't make more of an effort to reach students on an emotional level. We must think of a student as a whole person, made up of intellect, reason, and emotion. Often our communication aimed at the feelings and sensitivities of our students has greater impact than does class content aimed at their intellect.

For most teachers with over fifteen years experience in the classroom, the school environment is so completely altered from what it was prior to the late 1960's that it is hardly recognizable. Our schools currently serve children with Arabic, Asian, American Indian, Hispanic, and Ethiopian, as well as black and white American backgrounds. To guarantee these students an adequate educational opportunity, the federal government has mandated programs of English as a Second Language and Bilingual Education in public schools. These programs don't necessarily reach the child's psyche. As impressionable as all children are, it is important to deal with their emotional as well as scholastic needs. To ensure academic progress and social integration, the schools need to focus on the self-esteem needs of all these students. Teachers are able to be a positive force in the building of healthy self-images in school children. By understanding and accepting each child as a worthwhile, competent individual, the classroom teacher will aid the child in fostering a confident and self-affirming view of him or herself.

We are able, through our verbal and nonverbal communication behaviors, to instill feelings of self-worth and reinforce positive self-images within the youngsters we teach. The ideas that follow are specific suggestions that are easy to accomplish. Begin with these basic positive behaviors:

1) *Eye contact.* Nothing demonstrates a friendly greeting or brings about personal rapport faster than direct eye contact. Diverting our gaze from a student can lead to misinterpretations and negative perceptions.

2) *Smile.* A warm, genuine, open smile is a clear indication of accepting behavior. Help the students to feel welcome and secure.

3) *Pronounce names correctly.* Nothing is as disheartening as hearing one's name mispronounced. A few years ago a young Hispanic student was experiencing difficulty with a teacher who insisted on calling him Joe instead of Jose. Hearing his name Americanized was perceived as demeaning by Jose. If the teacher had been sensitive to the student's feelings from the start, a positive relationship, instead of a struggle, might have ensued. Most schools have counselors and teachers in the Bilingual Program who will gladly help you with difficult or unusual pronunciations.

4) *Be patient.* These students are adjusting to a new language. The content of your courses, the method of your teaching style, homework, and classwork are yet other dimensions to which they must adjust.

5) *Use clear, concrete objectives for classwork and homework assignments.* In order to comprehend content, it is necessary to remove ambiguity in assignments or goals of specific units.

6) *Be sensitive to cultural differences.* Classroom teachers today must be aware and accepting of a variety of modes of dress, behavior, attitudes, and values that are present in the students they teach. I was on my way to my first class in the morning when

another teacher approached me complaining of the stench in his classroom. How could anyone eat garlic in the morning, he wondered. It was going to be a very long year for this teacher. Each child must feel that he or she is in a supportive, welcoming environment for self-worth to materialize. Allow your students to teach you about their backgrounds and experiences. This will make them feel important and they will sense your genuine interest. A rapport with your school's bilingual teachers will help you in understanding the cultural background of many of these language minority children.

To ensure success of our curricula, lesson plans, counseling sessions, testing programs, and mastery learning methods, a positive self-image must be fostered in all our students. Bilingual and monolingual minority children who are English-deficient in a primarily English-speaking nation may require special attention to the six strategies listed here. In order to enhance self-esteem in these students, we all need to work toward awareness, sensitivity and acceptance of cultural differences.

Fred Garbowitz

Improving Performance By Maximizing Feedback For Native And Non-Native Speakers Of English

Goal: To maximize constructive criticism and create an atmosphere in which students are receptive to it.

In today's multilingual society, teachers of speech communication need to encourage both native and non-native speakers of English to participate actively in classroom activities. Students who are from other cultures, unaccustomed to American education, may feel particularly apprehensive in some public speaking situations. This exercise may help to reduce anxiety among non-native English speakers and should facilitate their progress in using spoken English. Furthermore, their comments in follow-up discussions will provide the instructor with information on how well they are mastering course content, and how well they are using English in the new cultural milieu.

After each student presents a speech in my class, my students must be prepared to give at least one suggestion and one strength which they observed in the speech. I call on some of the students to express their evaluations aloud. Then I encourage the speaker and other class members to discuss their reactions to the evaluations. (Students might be requested to prepare their evaluations of speakers in accordance with more specific guidelines. For example, one part of the audience might be asked to focus on content while the other students prepare comments on voice.) Different variations of this exercise may be designed to meet specific needs of classes. The essential ingredient is that students are REQUIRED to express aloud both commendable features and suggestions, as part of an overall assessment of speaker performance.

Student reluctance at voicing criticism of their peers is reduced significantly because they know each member of the class *must* be ready after each speech to express one suggestion. Similarly, students to whom recommendations for improvement are made are less likely to feel embarrassed by, or resent, any suggestions. All students are receiving suggestions. No student is being singled out. No member of the audience is perceived as being excessively critical. In short, everyone must give and receive constructive criticism in the class.

As students feel more comfortable about providing feedback, instructors can assess the nature of the feedback more methodically. This assessment should provide some measure of the degree to which students are achieving the objectives established for the course. Additionally, since students must express their suggestions aloud, their choice of language and manner of expression should reveal their growing interpersonal communication skills. Their ability to participate in follow-up discussions of their evaluative comments should indicate the depth of their knowledge of the subject matter, and should provide further evidence of their interpersonal communication skills.

Undoubtedly, many speech instructors use a technique similar to this one. Perhaps they have not been aware of the added significance of the technique in multilingual-multicultural settings, where non-native English speakers learn to accept this requirement as an expectation of the instructor—and as a requirement of the class. These students dicover that oral English proficiency becomes part of all interpersonal classroom encounters experienced during evaluation sessions in the speech communication class.

Martin R. Gitterman

A Native American Speech Text for Classroom Use

Goal: To broaden student ideas about what constitutes effective communication by exposing them to public speaking not ordinarily studied in the basic course.

In the past most of the speeches studied in the introductory course were delivered by white males. Thankfully, we have begun to broaden our examples to include more speeches by minorities and women, but even these tend to represent a "mainstream" approach to the communicative act.

Over the years, I have had success using a greater variety of public address than one usually finds provided in the textbooks. One particular example is a speech by the American Indian spokesman Sa-go-ye-wat-ha, or Red Jacket. Red Jacket was prominent during the early years of the nineteenth century, when he defended the Seneca Indians against whites who were encroaching upon tribal lands and trying to change their way of life.

The Senecas were one of six members of the Iroquois Confederacy, and over the years they developed a reputation as "forest diplomats" during meetings with representatives from France, Britain, and the infant United States. Public speakers were absolutely necessary to the Iroquois in their dealings with outsiders and each other, and over the years they developed a distinctive and effective communication style. Today, Iroquois speakers continue to defend Confederacy concerns and appear frequently as spokespersons for Native American groups.

Red Jacket was probably the greatest of the Iroquois orators. Even though he delivered his speeches in the Seneca language, he was ably translated by the public interpreter, Jasper Parrish, and those translations were carefully preserved by white admirers. In addition to the speech texts themselves, we have a great deal of information about how the speeches were delivered. Taken as a group, the surviving examples of Red Jacket's speaking clearly testify to his skills.

Perhaps Red Jacket's best speech, and certainly his most widely known, is his Reply to Reverend Cram. In the speech, he summarized the way whites had previously treated Indians, and he explained that the Senecas, before they adopted Christianity, would wait to see how white Christians behaved towards them. Over the years, the themes Red Jacket developed in this speech reappeared in the oratory of other minority speakers.

Teachers who wish to include Red Jacket in their course should find the task relatively easy. The Iroquois have had a great deal written about them. One accessible source is Harvey Arden's article "The Fire That Never Dies," from the September 1987 *National Geographic*. Arden stresses the continuing contributions being made by Iroquois speakers. A number of articles and books on Red Jacket also exist, including an entry in the *Dictionary of American Biography*. Sutton's *Speech Index* lists a number of sources for the Reply to Revered Cram.

Harry Robie

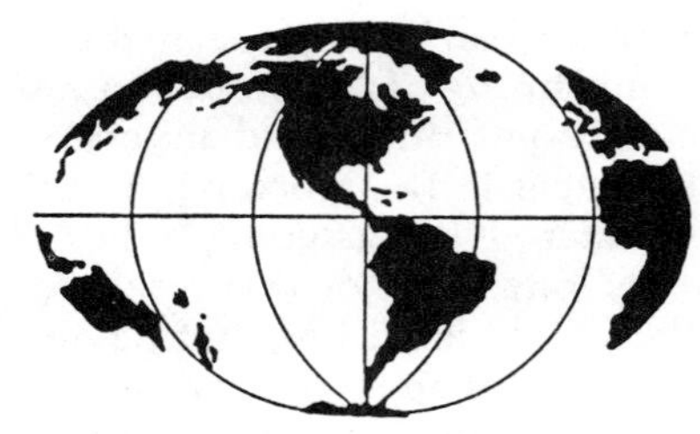

Suggestions for Teaching International Students

Goal: To assist international students to participate successfully in meaningful oral discourse by using a variety of teaching strategies.

According to the TESOL *Newsletter* of February, 1987, as of 1986 over 345,000 international students were enrolled in United States colleges and universities. These students are finding their way into our speech courses, bringing with them unique perspectives, backgrounds and needs.

Our speech courses offer foreign students more than public address skills because they immerse these students almost immediately in meaningful discourse in English language, both as speakers and listeners. These courses offer opportunities for social interaction through repeated practical opportunities in interpersonal, and thus, intercultural communication in the classroom. As a result, our international students bring us new challenges and rewards.

Some instructors may be inexperienced in dealing with international students. Perhaps they will find the following teaching strategies useful for enhancing the learning capabilities of these students.

Use both oral and written directions for assignments. Reading comprehension often is higher among foreign students than listening comprehension. Thus, by supplementing oral instructions with written ones, we limit misunderstandings that may occur because international students still are becoming accustomed to American speaking rates, idioms, inflections, and so on.

Incorporate a variety of teaching methods to accommodate different habits of learning. According to Joy M. Reid (*TESOL Quarterly*, March 1987) certain English As A Second Language (ESL) students have learning style preferences, based upon their native learning practices. Koreans, for example, were most comfortable with the visual learning style. Japanese were significantly less auditory than Arabs. Americans were less tactile than their ESL counterparts. Reid suggests that teachers should use a variety of strategies to reach *all* students, including reading, lectures, graphs, hands-on experiences, experiental methods, and combinations of these techniques. Reading assignments and lectures on the persuasive speech could be augmented by handouts, group discussions on topic selections, attitude surveys, reviews of taped and written persuasive speeches, and rehearsal rounds with a partner. Reaching a student on as many learning levels as possible is sound pedagogy.

Be conscious of idiom usage. The literal translations of some of our idioms are quite confusing to international students if they are not aware of our meaning. For example, such idioms as "You're pulling my leg," "I'm fed up," and "Going out on a limb" may be misunderstood by many international students unless the teacher explains their meaning.

Modeling can be beneficial. Foreign students usually find observations of live or videotaped speakers helpful before they give a speech. These students must "switch codes" in both verbal and nonverbal communication. Knowing another language is not enough to communicate effectively. However, you should emphasize that adapting to the American environment doesn't mean students are foresaking their own heritage. This simply is a method of adapting the message to the audience. It might be helpful to have a class discussion on nonverbal communication which is culture specific. During this discussion, you could discuss appropriate and inappropriate nonverbal communication in the United States and encourage international students to provide examples of acceptable and unacceptable nonverbal messages from their own cultures.

Encourage group discussions. Have students discuss a list of topics, check outlines, discuss audience adaptation, and so on, in small groups. This group work improves the quality of the assignment while promoting intercultural interaction and meaningful communication. Also, by placing international students in groups to study for tests or practice speeches, you will encourage meaningful intercultural communication for both foreign and local students.

Encourage international students to choose topics related to issues and ideas of importance to their countries and chosen professions. We can ease apprehension among our foreign students by encouraging them to begin with familiar topics. Often, intercultural bridges are built with the rest of the class when foreign students speak about their homelands. Also, confidence develops as students begin their speaking experiences by talking about familiar things.

Openly discuss the fact that errors WILL occur in extemporaneous speeches. Both American and foreign students who believe they must give a perfect speech, will worry about fear and failure. Specific techniques and strategies to conquer apprehension, combined with frank classroom dialogues on the subject, can be cathartic.

Allow international students to role play as they speak. Lizabeth England (*TESOL Newsletter, June 1987*) effectively met her ESL students' fear of failure by allowing them to role play as they spoke. You could encourage each student to assume an identity, such as an ambassador, tour guide, CEO, as often is done in presentational speeches. Once a student adopts an identity, that identity makes the error—not the student. Role playing frees the student to attempt to communicate in a meaningful manner.

When possible, correct errors AFTER the speech. Correction is essential to language improvement. However, grammar errors that do not interfere with message comprehension usually don't require a teacher to interrupt the student while s/he is speaking. On the other hand, if a student's error causes confusion in comprehension, a teacher is obliged to call this to the student's attention to help him/her get a point across.

Schedule frequent conferences. Many foreign students will not approach instructors to ask questions or seek advice. Conferences can provide an instructor with insight about international students. Further, students can clarify assignments and set goals. You may wish to refer international students who are having particular difficulties to tutorial or learning assistance services which are available on your campus.

If a major problem arises, schedule a meeting with the International Students' Advisor. Advisors to foreign students are concerned with the academic performances of their advisees. They also can provide valuable information about individual students, cultural differences, and possible alternative classroom strategies.

Be sure international students understand their success in the course ultimately rests upon their shoulders. The integrity of your grading system must be maintained by *all* students. Recognizing and appreciating the special needs of international students does not exempt them from meeting the normal course requirements.

Charlynn Ross

Helping International Students Adapt To American Communication Norms

Goal: To facilitate international students' communication by exposing them to American cultural norms and broadening their perspectives for sending and interpreting messages.

Effective communication is more than sharing language. It also requires senders and receivers to share cultural perspectives. Often, in teaching speech communication to international students, we emphasize building vocabulary, word usage, pronunciation, and so on, but devote little attention to beliefs, values, and patterns of behavior. We may teach audience analysis but fail to realize our international students' perceptions are culturally egocentric and therefore, different from American norms. As a result, misunderstandings and ineffective communication can result. To help break down cultural barriers, I have used the following activity.

Divide the class into groups of 5 students, attempting to separate students from the same or similar cultures. (This will help reduce the tendency of students to group together and reinforce the "rightness" of their own cultural patterns, and to resist "new" cultural norms you are trying to instill in them.)

Take one group per class session on a campus OBSERVATION/INTERACTION EXPLORATION while the rest of the class is given another assignment (such as watching a videotape which demonstrates specific behavioral norms and responding to a list of questions regarding them). This exploration may be to the cafeteria, student center, bookstore, or any other location where people congregate and interact. Students will keep written notes on their observations of people's behaviors. After a period of observing, take the students to a quiet spot and discuss their observations. This may include comments on portions of overheard conversation, distances between communicators, male and female relationships, and so on. This discussion usually covers things such as the appropriateness of observed behaviors, what the behaviors indicate, and how they differ from some of the students' own cultural patterns.

Depending on your location and the observations just made, you next assign each student in the small group a simple task as the other group members watch. Some examples are: ask for directions; find out what time it is from someone you don't know; join a group already seated at a table in the cafeteria. After each student has completed the tasks assigned, again go off to a quiet spot and discuss student reactions to their tasks. The rest of the students should be ready to comment on whether or not typical American cultural norms were followed.

The activity works well as students gain confidence in exhibiting a new cultural pattern in the "real world," rather than merely role-playing in the classroom. It forces international students to interact with American students, and vice versa.

As a follow-up, I assign a list of tasks students must do in the next 2 weeks. Students must keep a journal and record how they decided to approach the task, where the idea came from, what occurred when they did the task, and their evaluation of the interaction.

I have found this assignment provides needed reinforcement to encourage international students to change their cultural perceptions—as well as the "permission" some students seem to need to make this change. We need to remember that international students face 2 major barriers as they adapt to American culture: 1. Family pressure to maintain their cultural values, ways, and behaviors, and 2. The rarely expressed idea that many American ways are "wrong" when based upon their cultural perspectives of respect, aggression, norms, and so on. Yet, when we require these behaviors as homework, they become legitimized.

Therefore, since our cultural perspectives affect our interactions, it is important that we strive to share both our language (and the rules which govern it) and our culture, as we teach communication to international students.

Allison Schumer

Group Discussion

California Dreamin'

Goal: To help students in group discussion and group communication classes to understand the need for, and the role of, criteria in the problem-solving process.

One of the most popular activities in my Group Discussion and Group Communication classes is "California Dreamin'". The following information is distributed to students.

The individuals in your group are members of an exchange program from universities and colleges across the United States. All of you have been selected for a special Speech Communication Program being headquartered at (name of your institution). For now, your group's task is to find a house for *your group* to rent for the current semester.

First, you must come up with the criteria that your house must contain in order to best meet the needs of ALL your fellow group members. Thus, you must take into consideration pets, hobbies, parking needs, costs, and so on. Then you must prioritize the criteria as to its importance to the group. (Some groups may value the number of bedrooms over the number of bathrooms and vice versa.) The criteria MUST BE REALISTIC! The list of prioritized criteria is due at the end of the first group meeting. Each group member should keep a copy of the prioritized criteria.

Following the group meeting, members should secure current newspapers and real estate advertisements to try to locate the house that best fits their criteria. NO contact between members should be made regarding their findings. Each member must bring documentation for at least three possible "houses" to the next meeting.

At the next group session, the members will regroup and share their findings. Then they must decide on the house that BEST fits their criteria. This decision will be turned in to the instructor at the end of the period, along with the newspaper or real estate ad that was decided upon.

At the final group meeting, each group should be prepared to explain:

1. How they arrived at their criteria and any problems they encountered.
2. How they arrived at their final solution (house) and any problems they encountered.
3. Whether or not the original order of the criteria had to be changed.

The life of the group is one week. No make-ups or switching of groups is possible. If you miss a meeting, you will receive a "0" for that meeting.

The practical application of this task to a realistic situation makes it helpful to students. Furthermore, its social factors make it an enjoyable task.

Cynthia L. Bahti

Pennies and Poems

Goal: To help the small group discussion students gain insight into the potential talent for leadership of each member within the group.

Group members often are not aware of the talents of their fellow group members. This can be a factor which impedes the group process, since the full potential of group members isn't used. Often, the person who talks the most and/or the loudest becomes the "leader." Sometimes the quiet individual is a better leader for a particular topic. I like to use this exercise when I discuss leadership in group processes.

First, I tell each group that they will need about forty pennies. Then I tell the students to see which person in their group can balance the most pennies on their forearm, near their elbow. (The arm is placed so the hand is pointed backwards.) The pennies are to be caught in the hand of the arm that is balancing the pennies. Group members are allowed to practice. Finally, the students are asked to select a representative from their group who will match their skill against other groups' representatives.

When the students complete the play-off, I ask them to write an original five-line rhyming poem. Again, I ask each group to select a representative from their group to read their poem. Ultimately, the whole class decides which is the best poem.

After both exercises have been completed, I encourage class discussion. Students gain new awareness of group members' abilities and bond together as a team.

Virginia B. Mayhew

The Group Process And "12 Angry Men"

Goal: To have students demonstrate their understanding of the group problem-solving process and decision-making.

As a teacher of the small group communication course over the past ten years, I have always had the problem of determining if my students really could critically analyze a group's decision-making abilities. For many years student groups in my class had to complete two major group assignments. The first consists of an observation of another group via a "fish-bowl" discussion of the NASA "Lost on the Moon" problem. The student "actors" in the observed groups are assigned roles to play in the discussion. Observers use the Total Verbal Output Analysis, Functional Role Analysis and a Lashbrook Interaction Analysis to evaluate the discussion. While these three observational methods are good at coming to conclusions about the quantity and quality of the observed group's work, the major obstacle to the success of these methods has always been the role playing abilities of the students.

At each university where I have taught the small group course, students have to take a basic communication course in order to graduate. They may choose either a course in public speaking or small group discussion; inevitably the more reticent students select the small group course to escape the anxieties of public speaking. Thus, I am left with a class partially full of reticent role players. The fishbowls lack the spontaneity, conflict and dynamics present in a "normal" group deliberation.

The second class assignment consisted of each group being assigned to discover some "problem" in the university and make recommendations for the solution of this problem during a formal presentation. While this is a good method to teach students the steps in group problem-solving (i.e., the standard agenda) and give them the exprience of presenting a solution in formal presentation, I have always disliked this assignment because it never really told me if the students were understanding the group process. My grades were based on group outcome variables, not the understanding of the group process. While there is some merit to this assignment—students must learn how to coordinate a group presentation and written report—it does not inform the instructor of the student's understanding of the dynamics of small group decision-making and problem-solving. This has created an unfavorable situation, but I think there is a solution.

I had often heard that the movie "12 Angry Men" was an excellent portrayal of group dynamics in action. After finding the movie at a local video store and viewing it, I knew that I now could create an assignment that would answer my questions as to whether students could understand the group process. The film itself is from the 1950's, but it is a movie that will stand the test of time. Twelve jurors are deliberating after a murder trial, and their problem centers around their efforts to convince the one juror to change his "not guilty" vote to "guilty." In its 96 minute running time, just about every concept presented in a small group communication class is acted out on the screen: the phases of group decision-making; destructive and constructive conflict; pressures toward groupthink; the demonstration of task, maintenance and self-centered roles; leadership emergence; supportive and defensive group climates; the use of a devil's advocate to check groupthink, etc.

I have created a "group consulting assignment" that takes advantage of this film to determine if groups can understand the group process and apply course concepts in their evaluation of this group. The instructions for the assignment read: "For this assignment, your group is to act as consultants to the jury in the movie '12 Angry Men.' The purpose of this assignment is for you to demonstrate your knowledge of group process by actively evaluating a group's problem-solving and decision-making. You should use concepts that you consider appropriate to this analysis that have been presented in class and in the text. There is no one 'right' answer to this assignment; it is your task as a group to demonstrate that you not only understand course concepts, but can also apply them." The students consider the following questions when completing this assignment:

1. What are this group's strengths?
2. What are this group's weaknesses?
3. How could the group improve its decision-making and problem solving?
4. If you were the leader of this group, what would you do to eliminate some of the destructive conflict?
5. Does this group follow the classical approach to decision-making?
6. Would a formal agenda have helped this group?
7. In what way is interdependent thinking portrayed in this film?

Groups must produce both an oral and written report explaining their answers to these questions.

To date, this assignment has given me a much broader insight into whether or not my students in the small group class are understanding the dynamics of the group process. I no longer sit and watch presentations wondering if the students really can understand the group process. This assignment has ended such worries.

Bruce C. McKinney

Making the Basic Public Speaking Course "Relevant": A Group Project

Goal: To relate the basic public speaking course to students' professional careers through the use of group process.

Pennsylvania State University's Department of Speech Communication conducted a survey in 1986 (unpublished) and found that a representative population of 7000 students ranked the learning of specific job-related communication behaviors, 65% of the time, as one skill they expected to learn in the basic public speaking course. Evidently, these students want to learn communication skills that are directly applicable to "real life" situations.

Because my students often question the relevance of enrolling in the basic public speaking course, and in a majority of cases, view the skills acquired in this course as applicable only to the public speaking setting, I developed a group project designed to: (1) increase the student's awareness of the course's relevance, and (2) illustrate how knowledge of public speaking concepts are practical and important beyond the public speaking setting.

This group project can be integrated into the basic public speaking course easily. It is assigned during the first week of class. Students learn to work together effectively and, through practice, to gain a clearer understanding of the group process. The project also provides an opportunity for an oral group presentation at the end of the term.

On the assigned date, each group submits a 20-page report organized in the following format. (This format may be modified to conform to individual instructor requirements.)

1. Begin your report with an interesting introduction that asks the question: "What types of effective communication skills are essential for professional success?" Preview your main ideas.
2. Answer the question: "Why on earth does this university require students to enroll in a public speaking course?" Cite credible sources. Include a paragraph about how each group member initially reacted to enrolling in the course. State your opinion and be frank.
3. Provide an extensive definition that describes the kinds of effective communication skills that apply to a professional setting. Cite credible sources.
4. Each group member will discuss and provide data, using at least 2 pages, that focus on the influence of effective communication skills in his/her major area of study. What types of communication skills are essential for your professional success and development? Research your major and provide credible sources.

5. Are the communication skills you are learning in this class those that can be carried over to professional settings? Why or why not? Based on your research, what do you need/want to learn that you are not learning in this class? Compare your research in your majors to your lecture notes and reading assignments.
6. Conclude by providing a summary of your findings and stating what effect, if any, this assignment had on your initial attitudes about enrolling in a public speaking course and the relevance of this course to "real life" experiences on the job.

After assigning this group project to over 200 students, I believe students: (1) gain a clearer understanding of the relevance of the public speaking course; (2) react very positively to discovering how public speaking concepts relate to communication in the workplace; (3) gain an increased awareness of the types of communicative interactions required of them in their areas of study; and (4) provide critical comments that act as useful guidelines for improving course content and that result in more effective audience adaptation.

Jerome S. Burner notes, in his *Toward a Theory of Instruction* (New York: W.W. Norton & Company, Inc. 1966, p. 5) that intellectual "growth depends upon internalizing events into a 'storage system' that corresponds to the environment." This group project provides an effective method of helping students to internalize public speaking concepts and prepares them for the types of communication skills that are essential for success in the workplace.

Mary Mino

Small Group Membership Contract

Goal: To increase group member awareness of constructive small group behavior and to increase member commitment to performing these behaviors.

This activity involves a short class discussion during which ideas related to productive communication behaviors in small group contexts is introduced. Group members then discuss these ideas further and create a list of expected behaviors. Next, this list is trans-

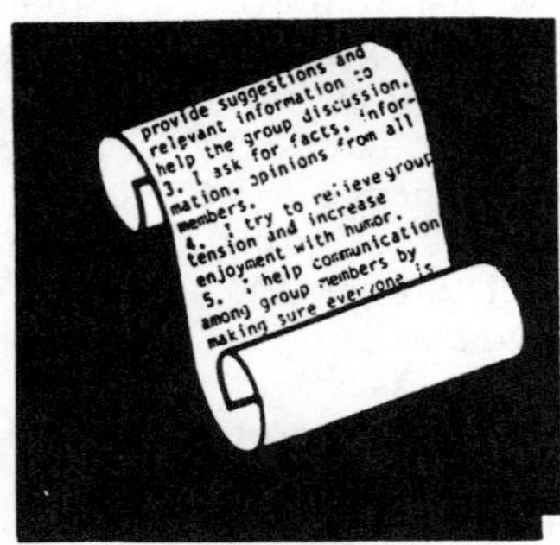

formed into a "contract" to be followed by all members on subsequent projects.

Before assigning small groups, conduct a short discussion of productive communication behaviors that will help groups to accomplish their goals. Avoid going into details; rather, state ideas and examples that focus attention on task and social-emotional dimensions of group communication.

Next, have the groups meet and discuss their ideas of good group membership. When the groups have generated a list of behaviors, have them review the list and rank order the ideas. Then have the group draft a contract that each member agrees upon. This contract should include: 1. Appropriate task related behaviors; 2. Appropriate social-emotional behaviors; and 3. Fines, punishments, or penalties to be levied for breaking the contract.

The consequences for breaking the contract may include penalties such as having to: apologize to the group in front of the class for being late to a meeting, sing a chorus of a song for missing a meeting, cook dinner for the group if materials are not ready on time, do the group members' laundry for repeat offenses.

Have the group members agree on the contract. One member from each group should be selected to type up the contract, leaving enough room for all members to sign it, and make copies for each group member and the instructor.

The next class meeting should allow time for each group to go over its contract once again, have all copies of the contract signed by each group member, and have one copy turned in to the instructor. Each group should read its contract out loud to the rest of the class. Next, lead a discussion of the commonalities and differences between the contracts. The discussion should end by stressing that the expectations of each individual are now clear and that the responsible group member should follow these expectations.

This exercise has proven quite successful for a variety of reasons.

1. It prompts group members to examine behaviors and consequences of personal actions on the group.
2. It allows group members to state their expectations of one another in a non-confronting, non-aggressive format.
3. It allows group members to discover common perceptions and investigate differences in personal views of acceptable behaviors.
4. It may aid in the diffusion of what could become major group conflicts.
5. Preliminary research and student reaction points to the conclusion that group membership contracts help to increase group satisfaction, commitment, and cohesion.

David S. Neumann

Group Interaction: Processes, Problems, and Consensus

Goal: To teach students about the problems that task-oriented groups face and the stages they move through when working towards consensus.

This exercise provides a concise and effective means of covering a unit on small group communication in the basic course. Students have an opportunity to experience the dilemmas and stages groups face when working on a particular task/decision. Two 50-minute class periods should be allotted for conducting the exercise and the discussion.

Procedure:

1. Divide the class into groups of 4-5 students.
2. Give half of the groups some newsprint, a marker, and a sheet of paper with the following instructions: "This group is to identify five of the major problems groups face when working on a task. All group members must agree on the final list. Write your list on the newsprint provided."
3. Each group of the remaining half should receive the same materials and a sheet of paper with the following instructions: "This group is to develop an original and comprehensive definition for the word 'consensus'. All group members must agree on the final wording of the definition. Write your definition on the newsprint provided."
4. Do not elaborate on the instructions provided. Announce to the class that they have until the next class period to complete the task and that they're free to leave the classroom to work on the project. Group members should not discuss their project with members of other groups.

Processing:

5. In the following class meeting, have group representatives from each of the "problems" groups tape their newsprint to the walls and explain their lists. Much discussion should ensue with regard to the fact that the groups experienced the very problems that they identified, i.e., defining the problem, role differentiation, inadequate resources, and the like.
6. A structured discussion of the process of decision emergence based on B.A. Fisher's "Decision Emergence: Phases in Group Decision Making," (*Speech Monographs,* 37, 53-66) flows well once all the group problems have been identi-

fied. Some groups may acknowledge that they experienced the stages of orientation, conflict, emergence, and reinforcement.

7. Have group representatives from the "consensus" groups tape their newsprint to the walls and explain their definitions. Discussion can revolve around the isomorphic value of the definitions. You also might include a mini-lecture based on J.A. Kline's "Consensus in Small Groups: Deriving Suggestions from Research," (in R.S. Cathcart and L.A. Samovar (Eds.) **Small Group Communication: A Reader,** 4th ed., Dubuque, Iowa: Wm. C. Brown Publisher, pp. 202-209) to help the class understand the dimensions of consensus.

Initially, students will be frustrated with the assignment and complain about the ambiguous nature of the task. They will come to realize, however, that ambiguity is commonplace in the "real world" and that interaction is an effort to reduce it.

Joe Ortiz

Interviewing

Using Self-Critiquing Techniques to Teach Interviewing Skills

Goal: To improve student interviewing skills by teaching students to critique themselves.

After several years of teaching the beginning course in interviewing and assigning self-critiques to aid student learning, I was convinced of their value but frustrated that they couldn't be even more effective. The usefulness of this type of assignment varies with the degree of insight students have concerning common problems of beginning interviewers, and such things as knowledge of interviewing principles, level of skill, intelligence, and so on. Supplying students with the knowledge needed to make their critiques better, however, seemed to involve instruction in common *errors*. I was certain this would have the undesirable consequence of making students more nervous than they already were as they approached the task of acting (many, for the first time) in the role of interviewer.

Then I found a plan that worked quite well. I simply hand out a list of "Common Problems of Beginning Interviewers" to use as a checklist for weaknesses and problems *after* their first interview is completed and students have begun to work on their critique effort. This strategy has worked, I think, because once the pressure of the interview has passed, students are ready to begin thinking critically of their effort.

I grade *only* the critique for the first two interviews. This further encourages students to adopt the desired attitude because the more critical energy they can put into the critique, the better their grade for the assignment. They have no need to defend their interviewing effort except that I've told them they are to include both "things done well" and "things that need to be improved in future efforts" when they evaluate their performance. So they can make use of interviewing principles covered thus far to look for strengths, and the "Common Problems" handout to look for weaknesses. Now, it seems *helpful* to them to realize that the problems they are experiencing are common enough to have "made the list." It also simplified my task of grading their critiques to refer to a number from the problems list, rather than write a comment. Discussion in general critique sessions, where we review their interviews, is facilitated as well.

Here is the latest version of the "Common Problems" list:

1. Hurrying through the opening so that rapport is weak, the purpose is unclear, involvement is low, and so on.
2. One-sided opening efforts in which care is taken to set things up, but the E (expert being interviewed) is given little opportunity to talk.
3. Too much informality; interviewer fails to approach the responsibilities of the interview in a serious fashion. The goal of a friendly, yet professional, atmosphere is not achieved.
4. Too much formality; interviews assume a very serious manner that is stiff and reserved, negatively affecting rapport.
5. Interviewer's plans are interrupted by E's "jumping the gun," usually while the interviewer is explaining the purpose or setting the agenda. E, being overly eager to get started, prematurely begins the body of the interview.
6. A tendency to dominate is evident; interviewer is *too* much "in charge," with little or no relaxing of control so that E has little opportunity to express his/her views.
7. Lack of subordination of viewpoint; interviewer's views are evident and affect E's responses.
8. Interviewer is observed to react evaluatively to E's responses, e.g., "That's good!" or "Oh, how interesting..." and probing suffers.
9. An inadequate sense of direction or purpose is evident; things appear to wander aimlessly, possibly due to a lack of genuine strategy or plan for coverage.
10. The interview moves along, but according to a fixed sequence planned in advance by the interviewer which is followed inflexibly.
11. Transitions are missing so topics run together and E is forced to guess, after the fact, that a shift in topics has occurred.
12. The interview is simply a series of questions, oftentimes with no effort made at followup.
13. Initiatives are things the interviewer thinks are important and that E is supposed to react to, i.e., "What do you think about X?" At the end, all we know is what E thinks about the interviewer's ideas!
14. Initiatives are simply too specific in other ways so that E

is "pinned down" to a particular type of response.
15. Initiatives are too long, complex, or otherwise confusing.
16. The interviewer is guilty of using "leading questions" or otherwise suggests ideas to E that influence responses given.
17. The interviewer seems preoccupied—whatever E says is "Okay" because the interviewer is busy thinking of what to do next.
18 Inadequate followup because the interviewer is ill-prepared to followup on E's responses, perhaps even misunderstanding E's responses.
19. E is unable or unwilling to respond and the interviewer is at a loss as to how to proceed at this point.
20. The followup appears to be pre-planned; there may be a glaring lack of appropriateness between the attempted followup and E's response.
21. Overuse of paraphrasing; the interviewer's main concern is clarity of conclusions; amplifying probes are not attempted.
22. Ambiguity, vagueness, apparent inconsistency or contradiction is ignored.
23. Depth is sacrificed to coverage. Only a single focus to each point is pursued and then a new point is initiated.
24. Failure to recognize or plan for time constraints produces problems such as uneveness of coverage.
25. At the conclusion of the interview, the interviewer is unable to bring things smoothly to a wrapup and "exit" line.

Roger Garrett

Helping Students Discover Interviewing Skills

Goal: To help students discover their own interviewing skills.

It used to be that confidence, while using a conversational approach to conducting semi-structured interviews, was a seldom realized goal for all but a few students in my interviewing classes. I began to realize that a second course would be needed to develop a degree of genuine competence. Then I started assigning a series of out-of-class conversations as mini-learning experiences and found it greatly increased desired results during one quarter. Now the exceptions are the ones who *haven't* developed real knowledge, skill, and confidence by the end of the class!

Rather than trying to talk to students about skills yet to be developed, I use these out-of-class assignments to lead students to discover skills they *already* possess. They only need to sharpen and refine them when adapting them to the tasks of conducting an interview. These assignments, carried out unobtrusively within ordinary conversations with friends, give important opportunities for real life practice.

Three assignments have proven especially useful thus far. The first deals with an interviewer's need to maintain subordination of viewpoint. The second identifies skills associated with probing. The third includes activities related to initiating topics for discussion and making transitions between topics.

Assignment One. Since interviewers must be able to practice subordination of viewpoint, the first assignment requires students to engage in a conversation with someone who has a different opinion from their own, i.e., a potential for disagreement exists. At least for a couple of minutes, the students *attempt* to keep their own opinions and reactions to the other person's views to themselves. I don't discuss *how* this subordination should be accomplished. I want students to experience the challenge of subordinating their viewpoints, but also to realize how much their ordinary conversations require them to contrast their views with those of their conversational partners. This is especially important for students who typically reveal their opinions quickly.

I require a short (half-page to 1-page), thoughtful analysis paper of what happened in the conversations. This written assignment creates a "deadline" and also causes the assigned conversations to be taken more seriously.

Later, when discussing the subordination assignment, we emphasize that maintaining subordination of viewpoint is *best* solved by the practice of *active listening:* focusing on the other's views and seeking to probe into *what* they are saying as well as *why* they are saying it. Their experiences serve as a rich source of insights into the process of communication that helps to reveal the special nature of interviews as they involve subordination. Students now *understand* what was discussed in an earlier lecture on subordination. Equally important, they hear their classmates express both frustrations and satisfactions associated with subordination. As a result, it is not an artificially imposed constraint upon their usual approaches to communication. It is now, to some degree, an emergent insight into interviewing as a communication process.

Assignment Two. I have found it helpful to lecture on the need for achieving depth and validity in interviews before I give assignment two. This prepares students to recognize the concept of "probing" as *active listening,* coupled with techniques that help to accomplish depth of understanding. Then they complete a conversational assignment which focuses on probing. As before, I give no instructions on *how* to probe. When the assignment is completed, a rich source of experience and frustrations is available for exploring ideas, insights, and useful techniques on probing. These become sources for critical perspectives on suggestions found in more formal readings on the subject of interviewing. As in the first assignment, the discussion that results from this experience helps to clarify and establish important principles of interviewing. It also leads naturally to the next assignment.

Assignment Three. In daily conversations, participants easily move from one subject to a new one, or return to something that was previously discussed. Periodically, during interviews, the topic also changes in order for the conversation to shift to new areas. For this assignment, students make a deliberate effort to do these things and report on the results. During the discussion, the matter of "changing the subject" is related to *transitions* and the process of bringing something up for discussion is viewed formally as *initiative.* Once again, the students' own experiences furnish numerous examples of good and bad ways to accomplish these tasks. These may be elaborated upon to whatever extent seems appropriate.

My subsequent efforts to lecture on the subjects of interviewing skills and techniques have proven much more successful as a result of these out-of-class exercises. However, I am convinced that the principal benefit of using them is they reinforce the idea that interviewing skills should be natural and suited to the students' own conversational communication styles. The skills and techniques that will work best for them are the ones they have been acquiring and using all of their lives. However, now they will be adapted to the particular goals and purposes of an interviewer.

Roger L. Garrett

Language and Style

Language Awareness And Assessment

Goal: To help students become more aware of their own language, to learn to assess its effectiveness, and to improve its quality.

One purpose of most communication courses is to help students learn to use language more effectively. I believe one barrier to achieving this goal is the students' lack of awareness of their own language; they frequently have little idea of how they sound to others. The first step in helping students to improve their language is to make them aware of it and to help them assess their own language effectiveness. If an instructor does all the evaluation for students and requires no language assessment on their part, students may not become aware of the strengths and weaknesses of their own language usage and permanent change is unlikely to occur.

I have found that an exercise which requires students to make and analyze a transcript of all their utterances in an oral assignment is more effective in facilitating the development of self awareness and assessment skills than anything else I have tried. I have had numerous students who, even after listening to an audio tape of their discourse, did not recognize problems with clutter, clarity, coherence or specificity. But, without exception, when the students made and analyzed a transcript, they became aware of the problems. When I asked students to evaluate this assignment, the phrases that appeared most often were, "It was a rude awakening" and "I had no idea I said that."

I have given students a transcript assignment in public speaking classes, but I have used various adaptations of the transcript analysis in other courses. The assignment also works particularly well with interviews and group discussions. Regardless of the course in which this is used, the following steps should be followed:
(1) The instructor audio tapes some student oral activity and makes the tapes accessible to the students. I find students usually prefer to bring their own tape so that they can take it home with them.
(2) Students listen to the tape and make a transcript of all they have said. (When transcribing interviews, they record the questions and answers of both parties.)
(3) Students analyze their language, noting strengths and weaknesses, and answering specific questions posed by the instructor on a hand-out (above). Although the questions students answer vary from one activity to another, the above format for a public speaking assignment can easily be adapted to other oral activities.

I use this assignment in the first half of the semester so that students will have time to begin to work on language improvement. Making changes in one's language is a difficult, frustrating, and protracted endeavor. This exercise should be followed by additional work which will help students find, form, and control the language they use. Students' ideas are frequently imprisoned by weak language. When we help them to become aware of their language and to begin to have more control over it, we help them with all aspects of the communication process.

Sandra Hochel

Revising Speech Style

Goal: To identify specific characteristics of good oral style, and to give structured guidance toward improving style.

This exercise is for use in a public speaking class after discussion of the following elements of good oral style: imagery, simplicity, conciseness, creativity, subtlety and appropriateness.

The following passage is a badly rewritten version of the ending of Adlai Stevenson's address to the senior class of Princeton University, March 22, 1954.

> Time flys[1] here, *y'know*[2]*; soon you will be*[3] *saying adios.* And now in the *peace and*[4] *quiet* of this *neat*[5] *spot, get* [6]*off* on *trying to*[7] *find out what is true, reach for*[8] *the moon. With the help*[9] *of God,* you will take with you *long-standing, highly*[10] *valued compatriots.* And don't forget when you leave *that you had a purpose*[11] *in coming here — which was to become a humane,*[12] *educated person.*

Students are asked to identify the specific language problems in the above passage; then, rewrite

An Exercise in Language Assessment

Listen to the tape of your speech and then make a transcript of all you said. (For longer presentations, give a timed length for transcription, such as, "First two minutes.") Write down all utterances—even phrases such as "well uh," "you know," "I guess" and "and um." You are writing down what you actually said—not what you wished you had said or meant to say. Attach the transcript to this form.

After making the transcript, analyze your language using the following guide. When you are asked to mark an example on the transcript, be sure I can easily identify each example. You may wish to use a highlighter pen and then add comments in the margin.

1. *Using Clear Language.*

   Study the transcript and then ask yourself if you used language that immediately allowed the audience to understand you. Was the language precise and exact? Was it specific and concrete? Now complete the following analysis.
   (A) Select two specific examples where you effectively used clear language and mark them on the transcript.
   (B) Select two examples from the transcript where the language would have been improved if you had used clearer expressions and mark them on the transcript.
   (C) Revise the two examples selected in (B) thinking of a more effective way to get your meaning across and attach your revisions.

2. *Using Vivid Language.*

   Study the transcript and ask yourself if you used language that was interesting. Forceful? Did you paint any mental pictures? What special language devices did you use?
   (A) After examining the transcript, select two examples where you used vivid language and clearly mark them on the transcript.
   (B) Select two sections of the speech which would have been improved by the use of vivid language. Mark the sections on the transcript.
   (C) Revise the two sections selected above, making them particularly vivid, and attach your revisions.

3. *Using Language Free From Distractions and Clutter.*

   Ask yourself if your language contained any distracting clutter (e.g., "you know," "okay," "and um"), ungrammatical expressions, sexist language, or any other inappropriate language which could distract listeners. Also check to see that there is no unnecessary wording and that language is direct and compelling.
   (A) After examining the language, select two examples where you used cluttered, unnecessary, or distracting language and clearly mark them on the transcript.
   (B) Revise and/or edit the language used in the above examples and attach your revisions.

the passage, correcting the problems. The goals, are to help students go beyond a generalized judgment of the identification of specific problems, and to give students practice in creating better oral style. Below are specific problems in the passage coded to the elements of style under study. This coding is given to students after they have made their own judgments of the language defects and attempted revisions. After comparing the coded analysis with their own, they are asked to try a further revision.

1. Lacks creativity (cliche)
2. Lacks simplicity (unnecessary jargon)
3. Lacks imagery (very ordinary language); lacks simplicity (an unnecessary foreign word)
4. Lacks creativity (cliche)
5. Lacks appropriateness (usage is too informal)
6. Lacks appropriateness (usage is too formal)
7. Lacks conciseness

8. Lacks creativity (cliche)
9. Lacks appropriateness (a contrived reference to deity)
10. Lacks simplicity (pretentious phasing and word choice)
11. Lacks conciseness
12. Lacks subtlety (unnecessary final phrase which belabors and weakens the point)

After students have created their final revisions, they are asked to compare their versions, and then compare their versions with Stevenson's original lines as stated below.

> Your days are short here; this is the last of your springs. And now in the serenity and quiet of this lovely place, touch the depths of truth, feel the hem of Heaven. You will go away with old, good friends. And don't forget when you leave why you came.

The instructor may make the point that Stevenson's version is not the only right way, and portions of the students' revisions may be equally strong.

Marvin D. Jensen

Practicing Creative Word Choice With Dialogic Listening

Goal: To integrate dialogic listening with creative word choice.

John Stewart's and Milt Thomas' presentation of "dialogic listening" (see John Stewart, *Bridges Not Walls,* 5th ed. NY: Random House, 1990: 192-210) improved listening instruction immeasurably. Dialogic listening entails listening practices which feature active and creative exchanges between interactants, including focusing on "ours" rather than "mine" or "yours," developing open-ended and "playful" listening behaviors, and emphasizing the here-and-now creation of meaning. Dialogic listening avoids some psychologically troublesome baggage that comes with empathic listening. "Can one person share another's perspectives, etc.?"

I like to join experience in dialogic listening with learning about, and practice in, creative word choice. Students can learn creative word choice by developing flexibility with figurative language. I use a version of this activity in sections of freshman and sophomore courses focusing on listening and language.

As suggested by Stewart and Thomas, encouraging students to build and share mutual perspectives by interpreting and elaborating each other's metaphors ("Run with the Metaphor") can help interactants "co-build" talk and "frame" their experiences together. Developing students' abilities to use figurative language can also enhance their (1) understandings of the principles of language, (2) word choice in preparation for formal communication events, and (3) oral flexibility when seeking the "right words to say" in interpersonal situations.

However, I find that some students have difficulty understanding the goals of dialogic listening ("the fusion of interactants' horizons"). Most undergraduates also lack familiarity with figurative language devices. These two aspects make the teacher's suggestion that students should "practice dialogic listening by extending each other's metaphors" highly problematic. I have devised the following activity in response to these needs.

I prepare a two-page handout which lists by name, definition, and example, forty-five figurative language devices. I took the list of devices from Edward P.J. Corbett's chapter on "Style" in *Classical Rhetoric for the Modern Student* (NY: Oxford UP, 1965: 425-448); it is divided into three sections: tropes, figures of thought, and figures of speech, following Cicero as presented by Donald L. Clark in *Rhetoric in Greco-Roman Education* (Westport, CT: Greenwood Press, 1957: 83-107). I make the examples which illustrate each device as contemporary and relevant to everyday life as possible. Instructors may compile similar lists of figurative language devices by consulting English textbooks such as Sheridan Baker's *The Complete Stylist and Handbook* or Porter G. Perrin's and Wilma Ebbit's *Writers Guide and Index to English.* A sample of the list I use includes:

TROPES: the artistic turning of a word or phrase from its proper signification to another
Metaphor: an implied comparison between two things of unlikely nature that yet have something in common (On the final examination, several students went down in flames.)
Antonomasia: epithet instead of a name (I spent the morning in 102 talking to the Big Guy.)
Oxymoron: joins two contradictory terms (sweet pain)
FIGURES OF THOUGHT: a "new turn" in the conception of ideas
Prolepsis: forestalls objections (If you will bear with me a moment.)
Dubitatio: speaker pretends to be at a loss (It is hard to imagine how to address this difficult question.)
Aposiopesis: breaks off the sentence, but only after the audience knows what will follow (If Richard Nixon had known what would. . .well, suffice to say he may have acted differently.)
FIGURES OF LANGUAGE (SPEECH): verbal patterns which depart in ingenious ways from the patterns of everyday speech
Asyndeton: deliberate omission of conjunctions (We came, we saw, we kicked their . . .)
Anaphora: repetition of the same word or group of words at the beginning of successive clauses (I have a dream that someday. . .)
Antimetabole: repetition of words, in successive clauses, in

reverse grammatical order (Ask not what your country can do for you, ask what you can do for your country.)

I ask students to complete the following, generally as a homework assignment:

> Write four paragraphs and bring them to the next class. One should describe you as a person by discussing your most typical activities (positive and somewhat innocuous self-disclosure); the second should describe you as a person by discussing activities that you are involved in the least, things that we could say are "oddities" in your behavior (negative self-disclosure); the third and fourth paragraphs should discuss your position on the following two current events topics. (The teacher should select two topics currently in the news and list them here.)

In class, divide students into groups of three and pass out the "Stylistic Devices" hand-out, with the following instructions. Designate a speaker, a listener, and a judge. You'll exchange roles repeatedly, so don't worry about which role you take first. The speaker should choose any one of the four topics about which she/he wrote. Talk about that topic with the listener, but do so by using one of the figurative devices from the list just provided. The listener should then paraphrase the saying by restating, in his or her own words, the content of the saying and the feelings it represented. This should be done by using a different figurative device than the one used by the original speaker. After hearing those two sayings, the judge should create a saying, using a third stylistic device, which attempts to summarize what the first two speakers meant. After each person has spoken, take a few minutes to compare perceptions about the meanings which you were trying to represent with the stylistic devices you used, then switch roles. Repeat the activity until each of you has spoken about three of the four paragraphs you prepared.

The activity takes roughly 50 minutes to complete so having pre-written paragraphs and pre-copied device lists is important. Students sometimes struggle a bit at first, but once they've made and heard a statement or two, they seem to respond to the "playfulness" of the activity - a standpoint for dialogic listening encouraged by Stewart and Thomas.

I am able to use the activity as a springboard for discussion about the value of (1) sharing perspectives with others, (2) listening for subtle differences in images as represented through talk, and (3) developing control over a wider symbolic repertoire than was previously the case. This activity also prevents paraphrasing practice from becoming so much "parroting."

Edward Lee Lamoureux

The Slang Game

Goal: To stimulate consideration of the origins, functions, and importance of sublanguage among communication students.

Classes in many subjects include a unit on how language is modified by culture. Argot, cant, jargon, and slang often are considered as sublanguage which arises, because of the needs of particular subcultures, to serve specific purposes. While students readily may grasp how sublanguage both can facilitate communication and serve obfuscatory functions for others, they often fail to realize the importance of sublanguage in their own communication behavior. This exercise is designed to help students become more aware of the role slang plays in their interactions.

After discussing the cultural importance, types, and functions of sublanguage, assign students to compose a list of slang terms that will be used during the next class meeting to play the "Slang Game." Some students may complain that they "don't know" any slang terms, so it's important that they be given enough time to reflect on the assignment and discover that they do indeed have slang terms in their vocabulary. Encourage students to solicit slang terms from friends, roommates, and relatives. A varied and culturally diverse list of terms will make the game more interesting. Use of neologisms and idiosyncratic terms should be avoided. Explain that to qualify as slang, terms must be in general use and derived from argot, cant, and jargon of various subcultures. Phrases, regionalisms, and euphemisms are permitted. The instructor is the final arbiter as to what is and what is not slang.

To play the "Slang Game," divide the class into four groups of equal size. The object of the game is for each group to select words that the other groups cannot define accurately and to guess correctly as many of the other groups' terms as possible. Have group members exchange their slang term lists among themselves and select ten words that the other groups are unlikely to know.

Next, distribute index cards to each group and instruct them to generate a card for each of the ten words they have selected. Cards should provide a definition of the slang term, indicate whether it is a noun, verb, adjective, etc., and include a sentence in which the word is used. The instructor serves as "game show host," judge, scorekeeper, and commentator on the cultural and contextual issues the slang terms elicit. In alternating fashion, each group has its turn to challenge the other groups by handling the instructor one of its card to read to the class. The instructor should read only the slang term and its part of speech at this stage. (When terms are used in a sentence, they are too easy to guess.) The other three groups have one minute to confer among themselves. Each must write its guess on a piece of paper.

Next, the instructor collects the three pieces of paper from the groups and reads them to the class. After all three guesses have been revealed, the instructor should disclose the proper definition of the slang term and read the sentence provided by the challenging group. Since some slang terms have multiple meanings, correct guesses must match the definition on the challenging group's index card. A correct guess earns a group one point. If none of the groups correctly defines the term, the challenging group receives the point. The group with the most points at the end of ten rounds wins.

Students enjoy this exercise. The instructor is responsible for facilitating the experience to ensure that students see clearly the link between theory and practice. As the game progresses, it is important to use some of the words the students provide as examples of sublanguage concepts previously discussed in class. In this way, the functions and importance of sublanguage in communication become more apparent.

Richard McGrath

Listening

Listening Instruction

Goal: To describe the origin and current status of formal course work in listening at Lane Community College.

In the early 1970s, Virginia DeChaine became concerned about her own and her students' ability to concentrate on oral messages but found that few materials on teaching listening were available. She developed a one term, three-credit, college transfer course, using *Effective Listening* (New York: Xerox Corporation, 1963, 1964) and the *Brown-Carlson Listening Comprehension* test (New York: Harcourt, Brace, Jovanovich, Inc., 1953, 1955) as her primary resources.

As a result of student satisfaction, enrollment grew. Harold D. Sartrain's *The Relevance of Listening* (New York: Cambridge Book Company, 1975) became part of a self-study program in the curriculum. The increased enrollment created a need for instructional assistance (a "lab aide") to supervise tape check-outs in a laboratory (a converted classroom).

Eventually, the library secured additional sets of the program tapes which could be used in the library — or checked out by students. To insure that tapes always were accessible to students, copies, which couldn't be checked out, always were available in the lab. The following description will help you understand the current state of our listening program.

Speech 105, Listening, consists of three parts: 1. orientation, background and testing; 2. building skills of attention, retention, organization and note-taking (skills which are developed differently from the Sartrain program); 3. lectures and activities to improve "interpersonal" listening. We use no text, but the Sartrain workbook is supplied to students for a $10 fee to cover the cost of royalties and printing.

General Orientation. During the first two weeks, students receive an overview to communication and listening. They take the *Brown Carlson Listening Test*, Form AM now, and Form BM during the last week of the term. They view the film, *The Power of Listening* (New York: McGraw Hill, 1978), receive an introduction to the workbook and to the Listening Lab. Students must check-in once a week during weeks 3-8 to have their progress verified.

Building Skills. Classroom skill building begins with the original listening program developed by the Xerox Corporation. It is intended to teach: taking advantage of thought speed in listening to, and organizing, spoken messages (without taking notes), and learning to cope with external distractions. This program was revised but we continue to use the original program because the dated examples and sexist language provide points of departure for discussing skills needed to cope with internal distractions which hinder effective listening. The program has a student manual which we don't use. Instead, we supply blue books in which students write responses in the form of outlined notes. This is another way to increase our students' ability to take useful, meaningful notes.

Lectures/Activities for Interpersonal Listening. During the rest of the term we discuss basic communication theories which affect one's ability to listen to, accurately process, and appropriately respond to both verbal and nonverbal messages. We use exercises and activities which demonstrate how to improve listening effectiveness at home, school, and work. The effects of self-disclosure, values, perception, language, proxemics, emotions, serial communication, and stress/pressure created during listening events are the major topics explored. Several demonstrations of relaxation and deep breathing methods precede the final tests and the comparison of initial and final Brown Carlson scores.

Developing a grading system for skill building courses can be a problem. This was true for our Listening class. Due to the many variables which affect scores of any of the available listening tests, no reliable ways for measuring student improvement are available. After experimenting, we decided to use the following 300-point system:

Attendance: 120 points

Lab-Check-In (6): 5 points each or 30 points

Quizzes (2): 15 points each or 30 points

Workbook: 40 points per part or 120 points

The Listening classes have had a positive impact upon our students and department. Students claim that within 3-4 weeks, they see improvement in their grades which may be due to the fact they listen to instruction. They develop a greater awareness of the importance of communication and seek additional instruction in it in Interpersonal Communication. (Listening is particularly useful in giving remedial students some background for this course.)

Although we don't recruit or advertise, several vocational programs require Listening. Its enrollment has grown from fifteen to 400 students per year. Interpersonal enrollments have increased from sixty to 350 students per year. This additional, inexpensive FTE has allowed us to purchase new equipment and expand the services of our Listening/Communication Lab (now open from 9 a.m. to 3 p.m., five days a week).

The lab has sixteen study carrels with tape recorders, and two video stations, which provide services to instructors and students in Speech, Interpersonal Communication, Business and Professional Speech, and Small Group classes. Students use the lab to listen to tapes, make up tests, do assigned readings, view their video presentations, or for a quiet place to study — when space is available.

Mary C. Forestieri

Activities To Promote Students' Speaking and Listening Abilities

Goal: To promote improved listening ability.

Just recently, I heard a group of students of various ages sing and recite what they believed were the "real" lyrics of familiar songs. Not surprisingly, few of the lyrics turned out to be those which the songwriter intended. Examples ranged from "My Country Tears of Three" to "The Story of My Lie" ("The Story of My Life), and "No One Camp Pad With You" ("No One Compares With You"). Both performers' and listeners' communication skills appear to be inaccurate.

However, in spite of these mixed-up verbal messages, music remains a significant nonverbal channel of expression for young people. They identify with the point of view, openness of ideas and verbal expressions, and emotional intensity of the premise or arguments subjectively presented. The restrictions society has tried to place on language and behavior of the young appear to be overcome in many musical messages.

Many teenagers view the vocalist and the song as representations of their alter ego, and place the responsibility for their thoughts and actions on the "pop" singer as hero or heroine. The image of lone students with headphones, receiving direct and exclusive messages for their ears only, is all too commonly observed inside and outside the school environment. Can teachers use these nonverbal musical stimuli to promote more efficient listening and speaking skills in their classrooms?

The following activities can be used in an effort to associate music with communication skills reinforcement in the classroom.

1. Have each student write the complete lyrics of a favorite song. On a second copy, ask the

student to alter the words in a specified number of places within the text. Next, ask each student to read aloud, in front of the class, the original words *followed* by the new lyrics. The task of student listeners is to record on a piece of paper only those instances of change heard in the second reading. Students who have the highest number of correct responses will be declared the most accurate listeners.

2. Each student should prepare a paragraph introduction explaining the meaning (in prose form) of 2 songs from a list of 10-15 song titles which the teacher distributes. The assignment requires students to listen, outside of class, to the 2 selected songs and to create appropriate introductions or lead-ins for each. After the introduction is written, a symbol is attached to the back of the paper, identifying the song. A separate piece of paper is prepared with the same symbol on the back, but with a copy of the first "stanza" of each of the 2 songs placed on the front. Using a tape recorder (at home or in school), each student records the introduction as though the student is either a disk jockey, a vocalist, or the song writer.

Upon receipt of the introductions, the teacher (or the teacher and a group of elected/selected students) chooses the most appropriate introductions and plays the tape recorded selections for the class. Students should listen, without taking notes, to try to match the introductions with the appropriate song stanzas which, subsequently, have been distributed. Again, the highest number of correct choices determines those students judged to be the most accurate listeners.

A discussion before and after the assignment may be held concerning the criteria for an appropriate introduction, and the functions of an introduction to any type of text. The teacher may provide examples from various types of literature (novels, historical works, biographies, collected works by one or many authors, art exhibit programs, record jackets, and so on).

3. The teacher brings into class recordings of vocal music as performed by an international vocalist in her/his native language. On an evaluation sheet prepared by the teacher, students answer the following questions while listening to the recordings:

a. What is the mood of the song?

b. Does the singer consistently express the same feeling throughout the recording?

c. Does the choice of instrumentation and the rhythm of the song influence your feelings about the mood?

d. Is there a refrain or repeated section?

e. Do any of the words sound familiar to you?

f. Can you identify the language?

g. What clues suggested your answer to f?

The second time the song is played, the text either is sung in English or the English text is read aloud to the class. (If possible, a music teacher or advanced music student might be persuaded to provide the examples.) A discussion of the way in which the voice and certain sounds communicate emotions could then be introduced.

4. The identification of persuasive musical advertising messages may serve as another listening assignment. Encourage students to tape record media commercials and fade out the volume on selected message segments. The teacher can play a series of these commercials, asking questions about the gender of the main characters, the on- or off-camera narrator's voice, and the number of times the product name is mentioned. Also, a list of certain phrases can be given to students which they are to find on the taped examples.

A homework assignment may be added to include listening for specific types of product commercials, or types of media celebrities (actors vs. sports figures) and the verbal association these people express about their connection to the products. Having students identify the music used as background for commercials is another way that music and listening can be associated.

5. Recent interest in religious broadcasting and its persuasive appeal for a large segment of our population suggests that students might be interested in listening, not only to the kind of music employed on television and radio broadcasts, but also to the specific moments when music is used to heighten the verbal message, and to what effect.

If religious programming appears to be too controversial an area of study, the same idea may be applied to film. Students may be asked to analyze the use of music in recent films. A short film may be introduced in the classroom, as an illustration of the way music is used as a nonverbal communication tool. Students may choose any film they wish. Such an assignment can serve to make students more sensitive to the subtle manner in which listening and emotional behavior is affected.

6. Unrelated to music, but associated directly with listening skills, is an assignment which asks students to select an American who has made an outstanding contribution, through invention, research project, or creative effort which,in large measure, depends upon a person's ability to listen. A short paper is to be written, summarizing the individual's achievement and its relation to listening. Final papers than are evaluated by a teacher or panel of judges. The top papers are selected and students vote for the 3 top winners. The winners can be presented with gifts of listening significance, donated by local merchants: tapes, headsets, records, and so on. Community merchants may even be encouraged to participate by celebrating the importance of listening by sponsoring a slogan contest, or displaying student art work which calls attention to the listening process.

The more we strive to improve our listening skills, the more effective our communication can become. Using a form of nonverbal communication—music—which students find meaningful, may stimulate deeper awareness of the significance of turning in to the combination of words and rhythm. If a musical text seems to serve as a guide for adolescents, perhaps we need to integrate a study of this type of communication into our classrooms.

Enid Portnoy

What Is in the Shoe Box?

Goal: To demonstrate the impact of stereotypes, inference drawing, and assumptions on interpretation of communication with others; to provide an opportunity to emphasize the importance of listening and feedback.

I use this exercise in the early sessions of the listening class; it would be appropriate in any introductory communication course, and is especially applicable in a listening unit.

Prepare for this exercise by readying one shoe box for every 5–7 persons in the class. (If the class is

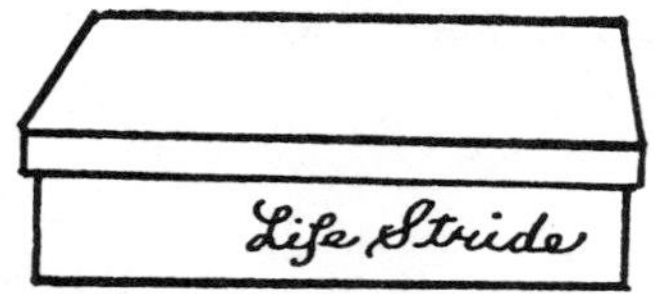

larger than 35, the exercise might work best if no more than five boxes are used with "demonstrative groups" while other observe.) Each shoe box should have a pencil-sized hole punched at both ends and on the top and bottom. I cover the holes with clear (not frosty) adhesive tape so objects inside the box cannot fall through the holes and damage the eyes during the activity.

I select several fun and somewhat misleading objects to have loose in the box—e.g., a large gum ball, a small piece of paper rolled to resemble a cigarette, and other small household and office items which vary in size and weight, and which jingle and rattle. (Be creative!)

Along the inside of the lid and sides of the box, I then tape other non-intrusive objects—e.g., cotton balls, paper clips, buttons, plastic spoons. After returning the lids to the boxes (closing the boxes), I secure the lid with a heavy rubber band around each box. The boxes are now ready for the activity.

I divide the class into groups of 5–7, and give each group one box. I request that each group appoint a note taker. I then instruct the group to determine what is in the box; they can rattle it, hold it up to light and look through the holes. THEY CAN NOT OPEN THE BOX. They can confer with each other, even try to convince each other. At the end of 10 minutes, the note taker is to have a list of the items which the group thinks are in the box.

After no more than 10 minutes, I collect the boxes and begin the disclosure of items. I try to use flair and drama during this part of the activity to enhance the final impact. I carefully open group one's box without revealing the items stuck to the lid, and ask the group note-taker to tell me what is in the shoe box. As the person names items, I try to identify loose items which come close to the description. I might say things like: "A ball, you say? Maybe you mean this giant gum ball? Wouldn't be to useful in a baseball game, though!" Or if the item is accurately named, I question them more closely. "You say a coin? Is it a penny or nickel? Nickel? What year is on the nickel?"

Once the group has completed their list, I show them each of the remaining loose items in the box; "But you missed the deflated balloon, the surgical glove, and the tinker toy." And then I turn over the lid and identify all that was missed there; "And what about these cotton balls, my blue button from my old favorite blouse, my sons' trinket from the gum machine? Gosh, you didn't do a very good job of identifying these items in box one."

I perform this type of routine for each of the remaining boxes. By box number five, students might even be a little irritated with me. "How were we supposed to know if you taped it on the inside?" they'll ask. I'll play this up, as well as every time they incorrectly identify an object and then say they *really* meant to say the item I select out to show them.

After all five boxes have been exposed, I look directly and deliberately at the students and say, "There is no way you could have known what was in this shoe box unless you could have taken off the lid and looked inside. Just as there is no way you can know what is inside a person's head unless you could open it up and walk inside that person, inside their feelings, their experiences. Yet most of you spent more time trying to figure out what was in these silly boxes than you do trying to understand another person. You see a behavior, hear a "rattle" and decide that person is stuck up, or that person is dumb. You hear a few comments and conclude the person really meant such and such. You see a person's skin color or hair length and decide they think this way or that. And then you never rattle or check back with the box again. Yet we all have a number of things stuck around the inside which many others know nothing about, but which affect how we talk and listen."

At this point I usually refer back to earlier lessons on the impact of "self" on communication and the role of projection on communication, and address how these even further complicate the process of interpreting what's inside the shoe box, and what's inside the person.

Students are usually all ears now; it is easy at this point to emphasize the importance of listening. I refer to this shoe box activity throughout the quarter whenever I can tie it to another concept such as feedback, trust and disclosure. Most students note this activity as the one which had the most impact on their attitude toward listening.

Roseanna Ross

"There is no way you could have known what was in this shoe box unless you could have taken off the lid and looked inside. Just as there is no way you can know what is inside a person's head unless you could open it up and walk inside that person, inside their feelings, their experiences . . . "

A Three-Step Process for Better Speaking and Listening

Goal: To help master a three-step teaching-learning process that can generate improvement in public speaking and listening skills.

Set, interaction and *closure* are the three steps needed to effectively teach or learn a lesson," says Frank Christ, reading and study skills specialist who directs this country's largest learning assistance center at California State College—Long Beach. Christ said this in a course, which was part of an advanced graduate study sequence in basic skills—study skills improvement, which I took at Appalachian State University in Boone, North Carolina in July, 1980.

Set means to provide a sense of the outline or sequence of key points in a message—spoken, written, or broadcast. *Interaction* refers to sufficient interplay of the audience in thinking about, reacting towards, or questioning key ideas of the message as they are presented. *Closure* concerns gaining a sense of completion of the ideas and how well they fit together, as well as reviewing them towards the conclusion of the message.

In my "Outline Mapping Plan for Any Informative Speech or Report," (*The Ideabook for Teaching the Basic Speech Communication Course)* Glenview, Ill.: Scott, Foresman and Co., 1986) pp. 22-23) I argued that the communicator is teaching a lesson in an informative speech or report and should use *set, interaction,* and *closure* techniques in sequence to get his or her points across effectively. Also, one has to do a bit of informing in persuasive and entertaining speeches. Hence, I now believe that any public speaker can improve by using this three-step process. Since a listener is primarily a learner of the speaker's materials, the three-step process yields three listening improvement techniques for systematic refinement.

The public speaker should provide *set* by previewing the main outline points to be developed in the body of the speech, after the attention-getting introduction. (Some exceptions to full previewing exist. In a controversial persuasive speech it might be best to indicate the general topical area. Also, when suspense about some subtopics is important to overall strategy, the informative speaker might indicate how many subtopics will be covered without naming them.)

A communicator can do several things in the body of the speech to promote sufficient *interaction* with its key points. S/he can speak at a slow enough rate to allow listeners to think about key points. The speaker should have at least two different units of supporting material (unless one very well detailed illustration exists) to give listeners more time and ways to visualize the key point being explained. The communicator should avoid coverage of too many separate points in one message. Too many points cannot be detailed adequately or taken in mentally by an audience. The speaker should translate or define technical or unusual words that might be a barrier to listeners' clear *interaction* with key ideas. Finally, the communicator can encourage stronger audience *interaction* with the material by having at least one attention-getting item, such as auditory or visual aid(s), detailed examples, audience participation, humor or rhetorical question(s) within each of the speech's major outline points.

Generally, the speaker provides *closure* in the conclusion of the speech by summing up the key points. The communicator also may call for action in a persuasive speech, or suggest how audience members can use the concept in an informative address.

Set, interaction, and *closure* also yield three techniques which, when used in concert, will provide quite a complete program of listening improvement.

First, a listener who is familiar with the four basic patterns for a speech (or any other message) can recognize early in a speech, lecture, or oral report, which pattern the speaker is using. Then it becomes easier to see which are the the speaker's main outline points and which are major supporting materials, minor items of support, or even irrelevant details. If note-taking is necessary, the listener will know what items need to be covered in notes.

The four basic patterns are chronological (time) order, spatial (geographical) order, topical order, and problem-solution. All other formats are synonyms or sub-divisions of the basic four. Identifying which of these patterns is being used provides a sense of *set* which makes it easy to see when a new main point is being introduced. This sense of *set* also helps one to remember the key points. A listener, for instance, might be reminded that "The speaker used a problem-solution order, talking about effects, causes, and solutions for the problem of alcoholism." A listener might think, "This speech was a topical order with five subtopics. The communicator first defined *schizophrenia*, then detailed three different types of it, and finally, discussed treatment methods."

Secondly, a listener should try to add an original fact, example, or other supporting illustration to as many of the speaker's main outline points as possible. This aids *interaction* by holding the idea more actively, longer in one's mind until it has had a chance to be stored in one's long-term memory for future retention. Also, each fact or illustration reviews the main point from a different angle, thus providing a fuller understanding of that point. Obviously, in a classroom situation, students are expected to keep current with reading assignments before a related class lecture or discussion. The readings are likely to provide a fund of materials from which to interject supporting materials to improve the *interaction* dimension of listening.

Finally, a listener will provide the dimension of *closure* by mentally asking several questions as the speech is concluding. "Do I understand and remember all of the speaker's main points?" "What exactly are they in my own words?" "Do they all make sense and/or accord with related materials I've studied or considered elsewhere?" Besides reviewing the full sequence of ideas, sources of confusion can be diagnosed, and they can be dealt with by asking the speaker a question or rechecking related printed material. New ideas and new implications of the speaker's ideas also can be generated by asking *closure* questions. This kind of original and critical thinking development is the ideal goal of our American educational system.

Most of us only understand and remember about 50% of what a speaker or lecturer has said in most situations. However, if we diligently apply these three techniques for listening improvement which correspond to *set, interaction*, and *closure*, I believe we may reach as high as an 80 to 90% comprehension and retention rate right after a speech or lecture. In a classroom setting or other crucial situation, we should look at our notes again within the same 12 hour period that we received the material. If we do this, and also visually review notes for related topics or chapters once a week, we may have to do only minimal studying for major exams.

Valerie L. Schneider

Nonverbal Communication

People's Court Comes to the Classroom

Goal: To demonstrate how nonverbal cues are combined to make effective or ineffective first impressions.

This learning experience is designed to highlight the way nonverbal behaviors can be used, either to enhance or contradict the image a speaker wants to project. Successful nonverbal impression management is particularly important in such work contexts as job and sales interviews. However, making the "right" first impression also is critical for social success.

The television program *People's Court* is ideally suited for providing examples of effective and ineffective impression management. Plaintiffs and defendants who appear on the program are not professional actors. They are ordinary people trying to make a favorable impression on the judge, courtroom audience, and viewers. The program is widely syndicated and appears five times weekly. This allows for taping and use in the classroom within copyright guidelines. (Copyright regulations state that programs taped for educational use must be shown within 10 class days and may be kept a total of 45 days.)

Before showing the tape, I ask students to form answers to the following questions while viewing the segment. Voice, dress, hairstyle, eye contact, facial expression and posture are some nonverbal cues that can be analyzed.

1. What images are the defendant(s) or plaintiff(s) trying to project? What messages do they want to convey about themselves and the dispute?
2. How successful or unsuccessful are the parties in communicating the desired impressions? Explain your answer based on the nonverbal behaviors of each.

3. What suggestions do you have to help both the defendant(s) and plaintiff(s) manage their nonverbal impressions more effectively?

Unsucessful attempts at impression management, in particular, can generate lively discussion. (For more information on nonverbal impression management, see Dale Leathers, *Successful Nonverbal Communication: Principles and Applications.)* For example, some speakers plead poverty while dressing lavishly, while others lower their credibility through poor eye contact and monotone vocal delivery. Following discussion of the tape, students form dyads to examine their own success or lack of success in impression formation and to formulate a plan of action to increase their effectiveness in future encounters.

Craig Johnson

Classroom Exercises For Teaching Nonverbal Communication

Goal: To help students understand, appreciate, and effectively employ variables of nonverbal communication.

Speech Communication teachers frequently like to use class exercises and demonstrations to help students understand how nonverbal communication influences senders and receivers of messages. The following activities may be useful for introducing initial studies of nonverbal communication.

Communicative Effects of Distance. *Horizontal Distance:* Ask students to pair up and to begin conversations while standing two feet apart. At one minute intervals, ask students to take a step back until they are six inches apart. Then have class members discuss how the distances affected their comfort, eye contact, gestures, volume, topic of conversation, and so on. *Vertical Distance:* Ask students to role play a disagreement between a teacher and student, police officer and motorist, or similar situation. Have students begin the argument while seated opposite one another. After a minute, ask the persons playing the teacher or officer to stand while the other member remains seated. After another minute, have the person who is standing now stand on a chair while the other person remains seated. Discuss and debrief the activity. (Students who play the teacher or officer generally report that, as they stand higher over the other person, they become more dominant, aggressive, and authoritarian. Students who remain seated report that they become increasingly intimidated as the other individual rises above them.) Discuss the effects of literally looking "up to a person" or "down on a person."

How Environment Influences Communication. In groups of five, have students look around the room, brainstorm and compile a list of all aspects of environment which might influence classroom interaction. Factors to consider include color of the room, lighting, furniture, arrangement of furniture, temperature, and so on. Have each group present an oral report to the class. This activity not only gets students to think and talk about environmental influences, but also results in useful suggestions for developing a satisfactory communication environment.

Why People Dress as They Do. Announce in advance that, for a particular class, students should come to class dressed in an outfit which is indicative of how they like to dress, and be prepared to describe in 1-2 minutes why they are dressed that way. Have students present their remarks. Discuss the variety of concerns (e.g.: people dress to express individuality and/or conformity; for aesthetic satisfaction, comfort, economy, status, and so on).

Impression Formation As A Result of Posture. Create a handout of stick figure drawings showing a variety of postures (or use photographs). Give groups of five students copies of the identical handout but tell each group something different about the person or context (e.g.: tell one group that these are drawings of a teacher; tell another group that this is a student). Give each group time to conclude inferences from the postures (5-10 minutes) and then have each group tell the class what it concluded. Note the similarities of responses as well as how their perceptions were influenced by their notions of the context.

Judging Personality Based on Appearance. Announce that, for a particular class, students will bring one or more pictures of people they know. Using an opaque projector, show the photos one at a time and ask the class what they think they can tell about the people in the pictures. Ask the person who brought that photo to comment on the extent to which the inferences were accurate.

Steven A. Rollman

Experiential Learning of Nonverbal Communication In Popular Magazine Advertising

Goal: To help students understand and experience how nonverbal communication in popular advertising illustrates nonverbal communication theory.

Since nonverbal communication is a primary influence in the human interaction process, I try to acquaint students with examples of it in popular advertising. I also try to make students part of the research process, thus allowing them to work with me in selecting examples of nonverbal communication.

In this particular project, lasting 7 weeks in a 10 week quarter in 2 sections of the basic interpersonal communication course, these are the 10 primary steps I used to help students investigate popular magazine advertising.

1. Divide the class into groups which would review a wide varity of popular magazines (from *Newsweek, Cosmopolitan, Rolling Sone, Readers Digest*, etc.).
2. Collect advertisements which exemplified nonverbal communication areas discussed in class lectures and assigned readings.
3. Compile the advertisements under appropriate nonverbal communication classification areas such as kinesics, proxemics, physical characteristics, touching behavior, environmental factors, artifacts, and objects.
4. Choose six of the most common nonverbal communication classification areas evidenced in the advertisements.
5. Photograph the advertisements in the 6 areas mentioned above.
6. Organize the slides in the 6 areas.
7. Write a script which describes the 6 most common nonverbal communication categories and how these categories were evidenced in popular magazine advertising.
8. Select suitable background music.
9. Record narration and music on an audio cassette which coincides with the organization of the six most common nonverbal categories of slides, using an introduction and conclusion.
10. Present the final product in class.

This presentation was completed during the Winter term of 1987. I used the tape successfully as an audio-visual aid to enhance a lecture on nonverbal communication theory in 2 sections of the basic interpersonal communication course during the Fall of 1987. Following the experience, 38 students were asked to indicate to what degree they agreed with the statement, "The presentation has helped me better understand nonverbal communication and how it exists within society." Thirty-seven percent said they "strongly agreed;" 55%, "agreed;" and 8% were "neutral" on the 5-item continuum. I believe this project was an effective means of helping students identify examples of communication concepts in everyday life.

James A. Schnell

Organization and Outlining

Speechmapping: The Road Through Speech Preparation and Delivery

Goal: To assist students to focus and organize their thoughts when preparing a speech and to sound conversational when delivering their ideas.

We teach mapping — visually diagramming a speech —in a variety of classes which require oral presentations (e.g., introductory and advanced speech, English, persuasion). Mapping enables students to prepare tightly focused, clearly organized speeches and encourages them to deliver their speeches in a natural speaking style. When we teach mapping, we begin by defining the *elements* that constitute a map. We then explain the *"how to's"* of map making. We conclude with how mapping can be used as a *delivery* tool.

ELEMENTS OF A MAP

Maps contain five elements: thesis, major points, sub-points, introduction, and conclusion. In order to visualize how the first three parts fit together easily, we ask students to picture a tree that has fallen on its side (tree trunk to the left, branches to the right). The tree's trunk represents the thesis, the foundation or basis from which the major branches (major points) emerge and give way to additional branches (sub-points). Lines connect the map's elements, thus enabling the student to see the relationships among them clearly. Finally, the student places the introduction and conclusion above and below the thesis, respectively.

HOW TO MAP

The mapping process involves three steps: formulate a thesis, delineate and develop major points which elaborate upon the thesis, and incorporate the introduction and conclusion.

Formulate a thesis statement. Preliminary to mapping, students identify a subject or topic area for their presentation, complete their information gathering, and analyze their audience, purpose, and speaking situation. Then they must formulate a thesis — i.e., what is the point they want to get across and how will they do it? We teach that the thesis should be one sentence which fulfills three criteria: a topic which the student narrowed down to represent the focus (limitation), the student's opinion or position on this topic (stance), and the direction of development the student will follow (direction). We have found that clearly specifying the direction works well as a basis from which to develop the major points of a map.

For example, we might ask students in an introductory speech course to prepare a speech about how speaking effectively can help them in various aspects of their lives. In this assignment, we give students two parts of the criteria — the limitation ("speaking effectively" which we've narrowed down from communication and differentiated from writing, reading, and listening) and the *stance* ("can help"). We also suggest the general direction of the speech with "in various aspects of their lives."

However, in order for an audience to know specifically what direction the speech will take, we encourage students to answer the question, "How?" Some students have answered the question, "How?" by suggesting contexts within which effective speaking can help them (e.g., socially, academically, and professionally). The student now can formulate a thesis which meets the three criteria we identified: limitation, stance, and direction. The thesis would read, "Speaking effectively can help me socially, academically, and professionally."

Delineate and develop the major points. After formulating the thesis, the next step is to "branch out" the major points from the thesis. (We recommend that students begin by writing the thesis in the middle of the page, on the left side, in order to have room to branch out their ideas.) Using the example above ("Speaking effectively can help me socially, academically, and professionally.") the student then writes the three areas (major points) on three major branches.

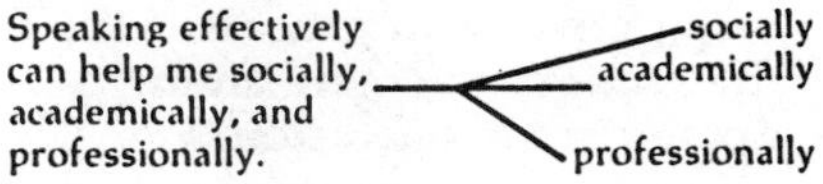

Speaking effectively can help me socially, academically, and professionally. — socially / academically / professionally

Having identified the major points, the student then develops each one individually with a more detailed map. Thus, the student expands upon the first major point by branching out each sub-point and additional supporting details as they relate to each other. (We recommend that the student use key words for each major and sub-point, rather than complete sentences.)

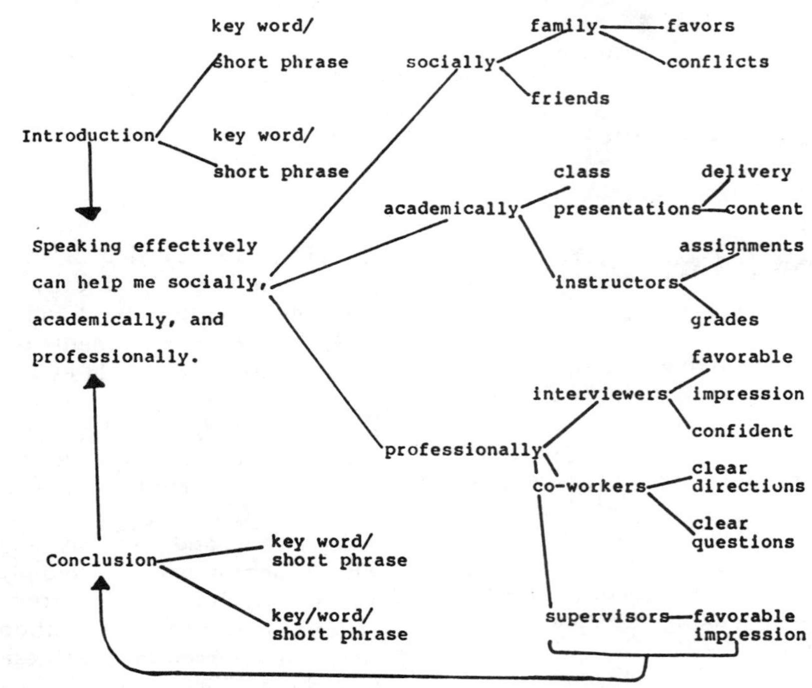

After the student has developed the first major point as much as possible, s/he elaborates upon the second. In other words, the student develops one major point as fully as possible before moving on to the next.

After the student develops the major points with the information available, s/he reviews the map to make certain that each element relates to that with which it is connected. The following figure represents this more complex map.

Incorporate the introduction and conclusion. The final step in the map preparation process is for the student to create an introduction and conclusion. Consistent with the frequently cited functions of effective introductions and conclusions, we suggest that the introduction should provide an effective lead-in to the thesis besides catching attention and holding the audience's interest. The conclusion should follow out of what goes before it by encapsulating the essence of the speech. To show the relationship between the introduction and the thesis, we ask the student to place the former above the thesis on the map. We recommend that the student place the conclusion below the thesis with arrows drawn to show that the conclusion relates to the thesis and follows the last major point of the speech. (See above figure.)

USING THE MAP FOR DELIVERY

Once the student has made a final draft of the map, s/he can begin practicing from it for the actual presentation. A map allows the student to see the entire speech at one glance; the student can see what s/he has already covered and what follows. This discourages the student from including irrelevant material while speaking.

Using a map encourages the student to speak in a more conversational style. Since the map contains only key words and/or phrases, it provides an opportunity for the student to elaborate upon each idea in a seemingly spontaneously manner. Usually, this results in a more natural delivery than if the student reads from a text s/he wrote out word-for-word.

Students learn the mapping process quickly and find that it easily allows for revisions when working towards the final draft. The map — a visual diagram of a speech, which presents a holistic picture —shows the relationship of ideas to the thesis and to each other so students can see for themselves whether the speech is tightly focused, clearly organized, and adequately developed. The use of a map also promotes a more conversational delivery style. Since our ultimate goal is to teach students to be effective oral communicators, we believe that mapping is a tool which helps us achieve our goal.

Brenda Avadian
Marilyn Thanos

Using Group Activities in Basic Public Speaking

Goal: To get students to work collectively to clarify and reinforce basic speech concepts.

Often some of students' dread regarding basic public speaking is the solo nature of the presentations required. When given the option, many students choose a group communication course over public speaking to avoid the trauma of being solely responsible for a public presentation. I have found that incorporating some group work into the basic public speaking class produces favorable results. Not only is the subject matter effectively reinforced, the students claim that their confidence and psychic comfort increase.

Two aspects of public speaking which lend themselves readily to the group approach are organizational strategies and introductions. When teaching organizational strategies, I want my students to comprehend that any topic can be structured a number of different ways, but that some strategies will be more appropriate and successful than others. The speaker must make a conscious decision as to which structure is most effective.

After discussing some basic structural strategies with the class (Lucas, in *The Art of Public Speaking*, suggests: chronological, spacial, topical, causal, problem-solution), I divide the class into groups of three to five and give each group a general topic such as "First Dates," or "The Use of the Library." The groups are given about twenty minutes to decide on an appropriate organizational strategy and to compose a few major points and subpoints accordingly. (In this one instance the students are allowed to fabricate statistics and examples to support their major points.) A member of each group is then asked to present these points to the entire class. The class comments on the clarity and appropriateness of the choices made.

The following benefits are realized:

—Students perceive not only that there are a number of organizational strategies available to them, but also that the strategy selected greatly influences the final product. (This is even more obvious when all of the groups are given the same topic.)

—Students are stimulated to think more creatively by being exposed to thought processes different from their own.

—Students get to know one another and feel less threatened by their classmates.

—Students get experience in front of the class in an informal highly supportive atmosphere.

In a subsequent class I sometimes use the same format to challenge the students to create compelling introductions. After discussing the functions of an introduction (Lucas suggests: get attention and interest, reveal the topic, establish credibility and good will, preview the body of the speech), I have them get back into their groups and ask them to come up with the most effective introduction they can for the speech they worked on together previously. They must be sure to fulfill all four functions of an introduction. They have about 20 minutes to work. Once again, a group member must present the introduction to the class.

I have found that when I use this exercise, the quality of the introductions presented in regular speech assignments improves. The students become acutely aware that their first ideas for introductions are often not their best. Having been exposed to some outstanding introductions, they more readily recognize a mediocre one, and are less likely to be willing to present one to their classmates.

Patricia Blom

"Spidergrams": An Aid For Teaching Outlining And Organization

Goal: To develop an awareness of the principles of outlining.

Students in basic speech communication classes often experience difficulty in outlining and organizing topics for speaking assignments. One of the underlying reasons for this difficulty is the misunderstanding of many students about the principles of outlining. Another factor is the apprehension students feel when confronted with the need to produce an outline. The use of spidergrams as a teaching aid addresses both of these concerns and helps the students understand how to outline and organize speeches.

Spidergrams consist of drawing a series of boxes big enough to contain one word. Because of the space needed for spidergram use, students should start the diagrams in the middle of a blank sheet of paper; these boxes are then linked together by lines. The boxes represent topics and subtopics, while the lines show the connection between them. For example, a spidergram for the topic "Types of Music" would contain boxes as follows:

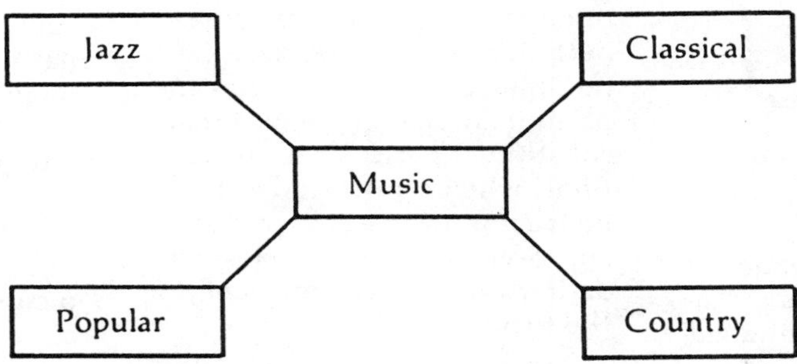

After selecting subtopics, the process would continue for each of the new boxes.

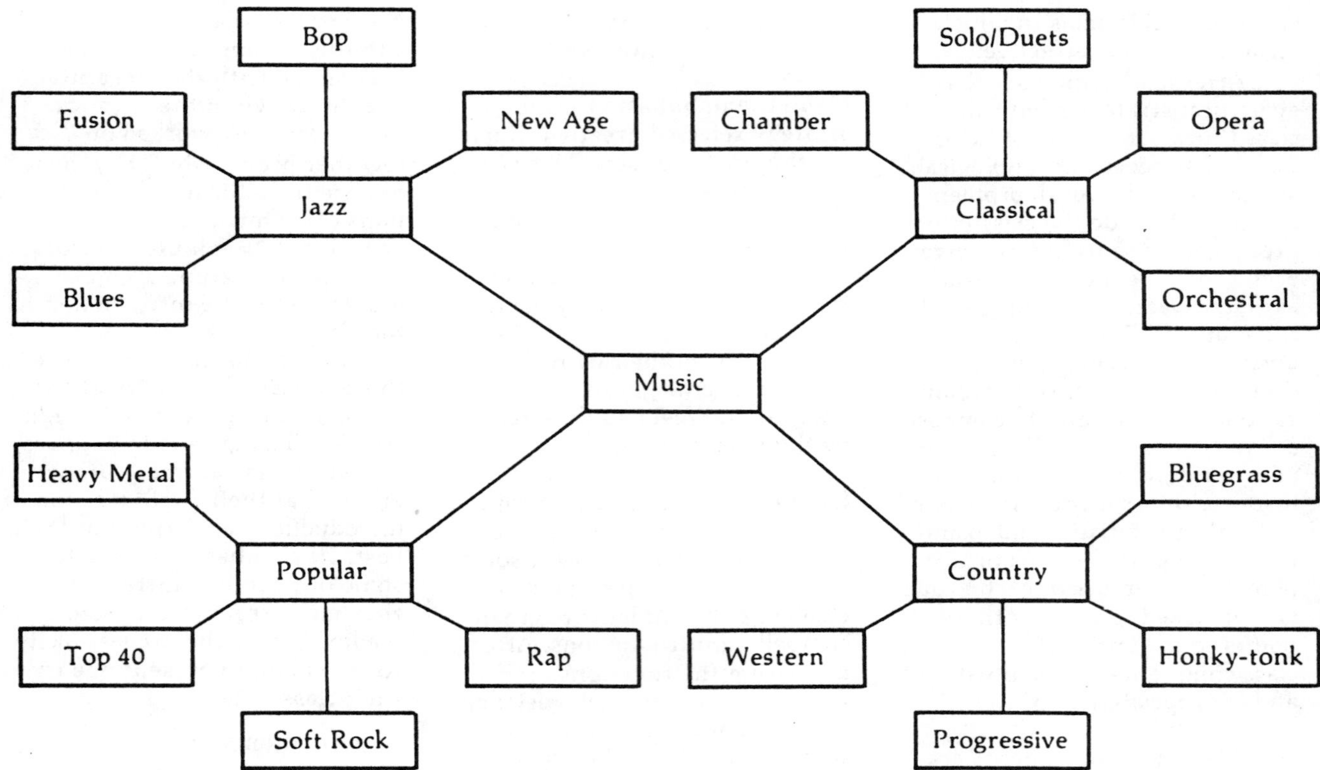

When explaining the spidergram, it is useful to draw one level at a time to minimize any apprehension that might result from being confronted with twenty-one unfilled boxes. The student now has a graphic illustration of a technique for out-

lining.The levels of boxes illustrate the principles of subordination and coordination. The instructor can use this example to explain the process of dividing a topic into its constituent parts to organize the whole. If the completed spidergram contains too many topics to be covered in the time allowed for the speech, it can be used to help narrow the speech and the selected subtopics can then also be spidergrammed.

When this process is completed, the students have developed an understanding of the principles of outlining and have actually "outlined" a topic. While the immediate goal of the students is to outline their topic, the skills and perspectives the students have gained hold greater value. Through this exercise the students have gained a basic understanding of the principles of outlining and have learned that outlining can be as simple as the natural division of a topic into its constituent parts. These realizations, when confirmed by the instructor, enable students to approach outlining with less trepidation and greater proficiency in the future.

Kevin James Brown

Outline The Pictures

Goal: To help public speaking students become more aware of ways to outline a speech.

One of the tasks for public speaking students is to create outlines for their speeches. I have found that this task causes some students great difficulty. For this reason, I use this exercise in my public speaking classes.

I have the class break into groups of 5-7 members. Then I give each group a manila folder containing 9-11 pictures of a similar topic. For example, one folder might contain pictures of women, while another folder might contain pictures of food.

Next, I tell the group members to divide the pictures into three categories. For example, the pictures of food might be subdivided into meats, vegetables, and dairy products. The pictures of women, on the other hand, might be subdivided into groups of blonds, brunettes, and redheads. The pictures need not be subdivided into equal parts. Finally, I ask each group of students to write one sentence about their subtopics. If meats were a subtopic for the food category, one sentence might read, "Meat is the main staple for most American people."

After everyone has finished, these students are asked to talk about how they subdivided the topic. The other students give feedback on whether or not they agree with the subdivisions. If they don't agree, however, they must come up with their own ideas.

I have found that students enjoy this exercise and they seem to gain new insight into organizing a speech.

Virginia B. Mayhew

Structuring: An Alternate Approach for Developing Clear Organization

Goal: To help students understand a variety of organizational patterns.

One of the instructor's most crucial objectives when teaching the basic public speaking course centers on organization. Outlining, one method of organization, has been described in numerous speech communication textbooks and is incorporated in a majority of speech communication classrooms. Although outlining is a useful approach to organization, students often develop the outline after the fact. Thus, speech organization leaves much to be desired. Structuring, an alternate approach, requires that the student formulate a residual message—the one idea the speaker wants the audience to remember at the end of the speech. Then, based on that residual message, the student constructs diagrams that contain each main point and further develops subpoints or substructures through the creation of additional diagrams. A structured speech presents ideas in a logical order—a progression of thoughts that helps the audience understand the whole idea.

Developed by Gerald Phillips, structuring's major benefit lies in its visualization component. That is, students are better able to analyze their ideas, see the speech's strengths and weaknesses, decide where evidence works best, uncover information needed to organize the introduction and conclusion, and remember their material. Another benefit is that structuring enables reticent students to focus on the management and manipulation of ideas, rather than on public speaking anxieties.

Although Phillips's explanation of structuring can be complex, understanding and using this approach is relatively simple. Because people have orderly minds, structuring helps students to organize ideas into patterns they and their audience can easily identify and understand. After formulating the residual message (When I am done with my speech, I want my audience to know or believe that . . .), the student chooses one of the seven structures by which to organize the speech. However, for the sake of explanation, I use an example that illustrates how structuring works by focusing on information-giving. This example incorporates a simplistic, general topic area (cakes). The instructor can use any topic area with which he or she feels comfortable.

Time—series of events or steps in a process; events or steps must follow a specific order.

Residual Message: When I am done with my speech, I want my audience to know that baking a cake is a simple process.

Buy ingredients
Mix ingredients
Bake ingredients

Space—parts of something and how they fit to form the whole either literally or figuratively.

Residual Message: When I am done with my speech, I want my audience to know that there are three parts to a cake.

Layer
Layer
Plate

Classification—information-giving is the speaker's primary goal; categories must be comprised of relatively equal, non-overlapping main points.

Residual Message: When I am done with my speech, I want my audience to know that there are three superior cake mixes.

Betty Crocker
Pillsbury
Duncan Hines

"Developed by Gerald Phillips, structuring's major benefit lies in its visualization component . . . . students are better able to analyze their ideas, see the speech's strengths and weaknesses, decide where evidence works best, uncover information needed to organize the introduction and conclusion, and remember their material."

Comparison—comparing things by showing their similarities.

Residual Message: When I am done with my speech, I want my audience to know that cakes and pies are similar in two ways.

Cakes	Pies
Dessert	Dessert
Rich	Rich

Contrast—comparing things by showing their differences.

Residual Message: When I am done with my speech, I want my audience to know that cakes and poles are different in two ways.

Cakes	Poles
Eat	Build
Batter	Wood

Cause-Effect—the speaker establishes a relationship between two events or a certain result(s) is the product of a certain event(s).

Residual Message: When I am done with my speech, I want my audience to know that when a person celebrates a birthday he or she usually receives a cake.

Cause	Effect
Birthday Celebration	Cake

Problem Solution—The speaker outlines a problem(s), offers a feasible solution(s) and illustrates the advantages of the solution or how the solution solves the problem.

Residual Message: When I am done with my speech, I want my audience to know that the problem of eating too much cake is weight gain which can be solved through decreased cake consumption.

Problem:
 Weight Gain

Solution:
 Decrease Consumption

Advantage:
 Decreased Weight

After explaining structuring, it is important to illustrate how to further develop each main point. Here, substructuring is used. The student examines each main point and, based on that point, chooses one of the seven structures to develop these ideas, as illustrated in the following example.

Residual Message: When I am done with my speech, I want my audience to know that baking a cake is a simple process.

Time structure:

Buy ingredients
Solids
Liquids

Mix ingredients
First do this
Then do this
Next do this

Bake ingredients
Baking times
Ready test

Substructures Used:

Main Point One—Classification
Main Point Two—Time
Main Point Three—Classification

Through the use of this example, students catch on to structuring very quickly. To be sure students understand and can apply all seven structures to different topic areas, divide them into groups. Give each group a broad, general subject area. Groups are asked to formulate a residual message and structure that corresponds to each of the seven structures. Each group presents this material in class. The lecture is reinforced through the opportunity the instructor has to correct any structural mistakes.

After using structuring as an alternate approach to outlining in my public speaking classes for ten years, I am convinced that students better understand the concept of clear organization.

Mary Mino

The Developmental Speech Sequence Model (DSSM)

Goal: To provide students with a step-by-step means of preparing and delivering the Speech to Persuade and Actuate.

As a speech communication professor, I have used a variety of models for teaching the persuasive speech. A common shortcoming of most models is that they require frequent additional instruction to ensure student understanding. In developing and implementing the DSSM, I sought a model which is detailed, but also allows the student a degree of creative freedom. The following outlines the ten main points in the DSSM model.

INTRODUCTION

I. OPENING ("Good afternoon. My name is. . . ")

II. OBJECTIVE OF SPEECH ("The objective of my speech to actuate is to persuade you to. . . ")

III. OVERVIEW ("The main points I will cover in my speech to actuate are. . . ")

BODY

IV. STATEMENT OF PROBLEM (What is the problem which you are trying to persuade the audience to overcome? Why should the audience be interested in your topic?)

V. STATEMENT OF SOLUTION (What is the solution to the problem which you are trying to persuade the audience to adopt?)

VI. STATEMENT OF RATIONALE (Why is the intended solution the most logical answer to the problem?)

VII. STATEMENT OF IMPLEMENTATION (How can the intended solution be put into effect? What *action* does the audience need to take?)

CONCLUSION

VIII. REVIEW ("The main points I have covered in my speech to actuate are. . . ")

IX. RESTATEMENT OF OBJECTIVE ("The objective of my speech to actuate has been to persuade you to. . . ")

X. CLOSING

My evaluation of these speeches is based on the DSSM outline, meeting the assigned 6-7 minutes time limit, delivery and adaptation to the audience, verbal and nonverbal factors, and ability to persuade to action.

Students have responded positively to the DSSM. An unexpected benefit has been that students speak with increased confidence, as they are fully aware of what is expected of them (but not at the expense of creativity).

Jim Schnell

Persuasive Speaking

Informative Vs. Persuasive Speaking: The Objects Game

Goal: To illustrate a major difference between informative and persuasive speaking.

A troublesome distinction for many students is understanding the subtle differences between an informative and persuasive speech. They are confident a difference exists, but find it difficult to articulate. This is particularly acute in a persuasive speaking course where students may not give informative speeches and thus, do not have the opportunity to observe distinctions between the two types of presentations.

I developed an "objects game" which helps to clarify one of the control differences in a memorable and enjoyable way. Although this is the primary value of the exercise, it also serves to illustrate 3 other significant concepts. In fact, if the focus of the course is not on persuasive speaking, any of these could justify its use: (1) the process of encoding images into words; (2) the process of decoding words into images, and (3) a "key" to reducing stagefright is concentration on the subject, not oneself.

All students are required to come to the front of the class where I show them an object of some kind that the rest of the class cannot see. The objects can range from the very easy to describe (a pen, paper clip, or ball) to the very difficult (a toy soldier, wrench, or an odd shaped bookend). Students are told to describe the object, without stating its function, until their audience guesses what it is. It is important to stress that they are not allowed to disclose the function. If, for example, they simply say, "It is used for

writing on the board," the class immediately will guess "chalk," and the dynamics of the exercise are not realized. After the object is guessed, students are to hold it up and argue why (by giving at least 3 reasons) the audience should either own or not own it.

Four things always happen. First, most of the students will come to the front of the class, look at the object and experience a moment of "Oh, this one is impossible," or "How can I ever put that into words?" The feeling is clear from the look on their faces or the first few words they mumble. These types of experiences create the perfect opportunity to talk about the encoding process and the difficulty of finding the right words to express what they see. This often leads to a discussion of how much more difficult this process is when they are talking about abstract concepts, the focus of many persuasive speeches.

Second, many of the guesses will be way off. For example, a student sees and is describing a plastic sandwich bag with the words, "It is plastic, thin, and has space inside of it." Students may guess "cup," "plastic fruit," or "spoon." This opens the door for a discussion of the decoding process and the way in which the same words have the potential to create different meanings in different people. Again, students experiencing the problem with these kinds of concrete objects can see the difficulty easily when language is concerned with abstract concepts.

Third, students from 7th grade through college seniors always relax, laugh, and seem to have fun when they are describing the object. This creates the opportunity to discuss not only the value of interaction with an audience but also the fact that they are having fun giving a speech, something they never dreamed would be possible. Then we talk about the feeling of fear that students had when it was their turn to come up. Almost in unison, they report the usual nervousness. However, they note that as they began speaking, it seemed to go away. I question where, as a speaker, their focus was. The students conclude that, as their time to speak drew near, and as they were walking to the front of the room, their thoughts were about themselves: "Will I make a fool of myself?", "Will they laugh at me?", "Will I have something I cannot describe?" As soon as they saw the object, their thoughts shifted from "I," and "me" to: "Ugh, that's tough," "What words will make that clear?", "That one will be fun," and "What is the audience doing and saying?" The difference, as they discover through discussion, is that when they are thinking about themselves, they are nervous. As soon as they start thinking about the topic, the message, the audience, or other elements in the speaking situation, the nervóus tension is reduced.

Finally, students *describe* the object from left to right, or in terms of color, size, dimensions, and so on. However, their description almost always is organized around spatial or topical considerations. When they *argue* that the audience should own or not own the object, they develop a problem-solution structure. Very often, they begin their argument with the words, "You need" or "You do not need" whatever the object is. Then they explain reasons why it is needed (problem or need). Intuitively, without any prompting, most of the students go on to explain how having the object will solve the need (solution or satisfaction). A few even describe what life would be like with the object (visualization).

Following the last speaker, I ask students to explain the differences between the 2 types of presentations. They recognize that both included information, but the first was informative and the second, persuasive. After a limited amount of prodding, they discover that a central difference was the organization (spatial/topical vs. problem-solution). We discuss how a problem-solving (or need, satisfaction, visualization) format aids in distinguishing between informative and persuasive presentations.

I have found this distinction an excellent starting point for clarifying differences because it gives my students something tangible to serve as a point of departure. The "objects game" involves them in a much more engaging manner than a theoretical discussion or lecture would and they learn 3 other important lessons along the way.

David H. Fregoe

The Premises of Persuasion

Goal: To acquaint students with a set of premises that establish the subject of persuasion as a principled effort, differing from other forms of "social influence."

To take the study of persuasion seriously, you have to believe it is both possible and desirable, also that it is genuinely preferred to other, less savory alternatives. I looked at textbooks on persuasion, seeking to find some list of premises for persuasion that would set forth principles distinguishing persuasive efforts from other approaches. While I frequently found discussions that dealt with the ethics of persuasion and sometimes a useful historical review of the break with sophistical methods, I nowhere found a simple list of premises. Therefore, I decided to develop my own. The following premises have proven to be useful for discussion at the start of classes, e.g., bringing the issues of sophistry into sharp focus, initiating fruitful exploration of approaches to the concept of persuasion itself, and stimulating insights useful to the development of persuasion strategy.

While the purpose of the premises is to provoke discussion, and it would be desirable to indicate some of the forms such discussion has typically taken, space does not permit going into that here. I'll limit myself to noting a Discussion Focus (DF) for each premise offered.

Premise #1. Common values exist between persuader and persuadee that can be made to support every genuinely persuasive effort; their denial or apparent absence only diminishes the *opportunity* to persuade. DF: The need for common ground, plus exploring the evidence and implications of some basic values (e.g., a concern for freedom, justice, equality, truth, etc.) being prevalent or even universal.

Premise #2. Persuaders have, or are able to develop, sufficient credibility to receive a hearing from persuadees. DF: The need for and various sources of credibility.

Premise #3. Freedom of choice underlies persuasion. DF: What are the differences between situations where there is an absence of choice and when choice is present?

Premise #4. Persuasion presupposes a condition of inequality, with the relative "superiority" residing with the persuader. DF: If there is *not* a defect, or at least a serious deficiency, in the persuadee's rationale for their position that is known to us, why are we talking to them?

Premise #5. Before persuasion can be accomplished, the persuadee must be made to experience a *need* to change, and this involves a discovered source of dissatisfaction with his or her present position. DF: The need for persuasive strategy relative to the identification of this need for change in the mind of the persuadee.

Premise #6. Persuaders must see persuadees as ready to change when properly approached on the issue. DF: It is the persuader's respect for the other person and a degree of confidence in their readiness to change that enables persuaders to resist temptations to resort to deceit or manipulative tactics.

Premise #7. Most people are reachable via a persuasive effort, and those who aren't generally deserve a chance to disqualify themselves. DF: What about people who are closed-minded, biased, treacherous, deceitful, or even evil?

Premise #8. The truth takes longer, but its effects are better and more lasting. DF: The consequences of deceit, plus a recognition of the persuadee's right to have *all* relevant information needed to make up his or her mind.

Premise #9. Any perceived threat to an individual's stasis will tend to produce resistance. DF: Again, strategy is needed. While persuaders *must*, temporarily, disrupt stasis in order to produce changes in positions, they must prepare persuadees for the disruption this causes.

Premise #10. Ends and means to ends must be weighed together; our minds allow us to consider them separately, but any such separation is only apparent and able to be maintained because of faulty or incomplete analysis of the issue being considered. DF: Some philosophical analyses of means and ends, plus the pitfalls of yielding to the temptations of expediency.

Premise #11. Persuasion is not *always* possible, true, but it is possible much more often than it is attempted. DF: What makes persuasion possible or impossible, plus how often do we see a *rejection* of persuasion in favor of some other influence processes such as conformity, obedience, bargaining, etc.?

Roger L. Garrett

Nothing To Fear But Fear...Or Is There?

Goal: To demonstrate how fear appeals are used in persuasive messages.

This class session is designed to dramatize the ways in which fear is used in persuasive messages and to introduce students to fear appeal research.

I begin the period by showing a short film that uses fear as a persuasive technique. Safety films available in the audiovisual libraries of many colleges work well for this purpose. Two that I have used are "The Uncalculated Risk" (a film on water safety) and "How to Save a Choking Victim: The Heimlich Maneuver." Following the film, we identify the fear appeals made by the film producers and list types of fears that motivate us.

After I have recorded 10-12 fear appeals generated from the class and written on the board, students pair off to brainstorm a list of advertisements that use appeals to these fears and others to sell products and services. Examples of ads that rely on fear range from American Express travelers' checks ("Don't leave home without them") to anti-smoking commercials ("One cancer you can give yourself") to laundry products ("Ring around the collar").

Identifying commercials that use fear as a selling technique makes it clear that fear appeals are widely used. At this point, I summarize research on fear as a message variable to clarify what types of fear appeals are most effective. Among the findings emphasized are:

1. Moderate fear appeals are most effective. (Messages that are not scary enough do not motivate listeners to take action while messages that are too frightening cause receivers to tune out.)

2. The higher the credibility of the source, the more effective the use of fear appeals. (Receivers have a harder time ignoring fear appeals from highly believable sources.)

3. The introduction of a solution or course of action strengthens a fear appeal.

To close out the class session, students use the three points above to analyze the effectiveness of the fear appeal commercials identified earlier. This can be done by returning to dyads or in a large group discussion.

Craig Johnson

The Key To Persuasion

Goal: To teach beginning students that effective persuasion requires a balance of Ethos, Pathos, and Logos

Why is the art of persuasion so difficult? Everday conversation relies on elements of it if the communicant is to be successful. However, students in introductory speech courses have difficulty grasping the requisites of successful persuasion. They tend either to bombard the audience with cold, hard facts, at one extreme, or to rely exclusively on appeals to the audience's emotions, at the other extreme. I had decided to eliminate the persuasive speech from the course syllabus.

Persuasion is power; persuasion *should* be fun. In sheer frustration, and after some input from colleagues N. Pfister, R. Sellend, R. Sellner, and N. Wendt, I created a group exercise in persuasion. It aimed at clarifying the balance of the three essential ingredients in any successful persuasive attempt: ethos, pathos, and logos.

The next semester, after completing individual informational speeches, the day arrived to introduce the conceptual framework of persuasion to my classes. Without any introductory remarks, I walked into each classroom and presented a speech entitled "Oranges Are Better than Apples." Despite occasional snickers and the perceived climate of student-audience bewilderment, my class was intrigued — and I had their full attention. Then I passed out the following handout.

STRUCTURE FOR A PERSUASIVE PRESENTATION

PURPOSE STATEMENT — Exactly what are you trying to PERSUADE your audience to do? Adopt an attitude and/or induce an action, i.e., X is better than Y.

INTRODUCTION — A strong *attention getter* is needed here; rely on *Pathos*. Also, set the framework by establishing an area of NEED, for X and for Y. Visual imagery is mandatory here.

PREVIEW — Succinctly but specifically state your claim (i.e., X is better than Y).

BODY — I The ETHOS ARGUMENT. Establish expertise and/or credibility through support and citations.

II The PATHOS ARGUMENT. Establish — visually and creatively — the emotional tangents of your position.

III The LOGOS ARGUMENT. Establish the logic of your claim through solid reasoning powers.

CONCLUSION — A strong *attention keeper* is needed here; rely once more on PATHOS. Also, be sure to summarize the highlights of your specific claim. (X is better than Y).

SAMPLE FORMAT — ORANGES ARE BETTER THAN APPLES

PURPOSE STATEMENT — To convince the audience that oranges are better than apples.

INTRODUCTION — Fresh fruit used to be considered a luxury of the highest order. We used to depend upon the immediate seasons and the surrounding neighborhood. Tale of the "Sailor Scurvey." Description of child with disease, etc.

PREVIEW — Oranges are better than apples.

BODY — I Doctors tell us that citrus fruits are the best source of Vitamin C. Support with testimony and statistics. (I have OJ each morning and eat an orange for my afternoon pick-me-up snack — I haven't had a cold in a year. My brother eats "an apple a day" and visits the doctor regularly.)

II Oranges are beautiful to look at, the color of sunrises and sunsets. Oranges are succulent and delicious. Apples bruise; oranges maintain consistency. If dropped, an orange rolls with the punches; an apple converts to applesauce.

III Oranges stay fresher longer (Support); Oranges are cheaper (Support); Oranges are easier to grow (Support); Oranges can be peeled by hand (Demonstrate); Oranges can be made easily into juice (Demonstrate); Oranges quench thirst better than apples do (Support); Oranges can be prepared in advance without discoloration problems.

CONCLUSION — Oranges are better than apples. They are nutritious, succulent, and accessible. Reflecting the joy of the sun, oranges are fruit-like symbols of hope.

I divided my class into groups of five or six. Each group had until the next class period to come up with a refutation entitled "Apples Are Better than Oranges." Students met outside the scheduled class period in order to keep their presentations as secret as possible. Competition between groups was inherent in this exercise. I encouraged creativity and strongly suggested that students use visual aids. Most important of all, each group's refutation had to match my speech, point for point, in the arguments posited under the ethos/pathos/logos section of the handout.

The results were gratifying and far exceeded even my optimistic expectations. I will summarize elements of two group products as examples.

In the first presentation, the apple pushers used a simplistic but effective approach, stressing the theme of patriotism. They also used a logical appeal for this product by showing that apples were available year-round. "As American as Apple Pie" produced a series of appropriate examples. A home-baked apple pie was produced from under a napkin for each audience member to sample. The group enacted a fourth of July picnic which ended with its members bobbing for apples. On Thanksgiving, grandmother received a basket for this traditional holiday. (Actually, the audience had to vote for either a basket filled with shiny red, green, and yellow apples tied up with colorful red, white, and blue ribbon, or a basket filled with oranges in varying shades of orange.) One student, costumed as a doctor, presented medical citations invoking the consumption of apples over oranges because of various medical reasons (e.g. less acidity, fewer calories, etc.). Finally, the group presented a dramatic narration of what the elimination of the apple would do to American folklore. For example, Johnny Appleseed, William Tell, et. al. would disappear from our collective American history.

The other presentation used the group members themselves as the supporting visual props. This group divided into two lines in front of the class. They clarified for the audience, through the lines of their script, that their presentation was occurring during America's depression years. The line waiting for the distribution of oranges was, initially, longer than that awaiting the distribution of apples. One by one, each orange promoter presented either a factual, emotional, or logical supporting argument for the choice of the orange. The apple promoters then refuted their allegations with a stronger supporting argument for their product. By the end of the presentation, the apple line had grown in number to five; the orange line retained only one student. A final note: the group's participants dressed in clothing which fit their perception of depression garb.

In summary, the final individual speeches in persuasion that semester were, in quality and variety, far above any I had heard in previous terms. Humor, combined with the balance of fact, emotion, and logic succeeded in illuminating the strategies of successful persuasion. I now use this group procedure as a precursor for any scheduled persuasive speech presentation, even though the format required for the individual speeches might differ (e.g. Monroe's Motivated Sequence, et. al.). The students have fun with this assignment. As with any successful group product, the results exceed the sum of its parts.

Madlyne A. MacDonald

Analyzing Persuasive Tactics

Goal: To help students determine the appropriateness of employing specific tactics in persuasive messages.

Students enrolled in my junior level Persuasion class are required to write 2 editorial-type persuasive statements in which they take and maintain a position on a controversial and timely political, social, or moral issue. In addition to the written message—and of equal importance—students must write a comprehensive analysis of the persuasive tactics employed in the message.

Analysis of persuasive tactics meets 2 useful purposes. It suggests to students that multiple ways exist for approaching a persuasive message and this recognition compels them to consider both subject and audience as bases for choice. As a result of the required analysis, attempts to plagiarize are limited. No teacher can be familiar with all the editorials and position papers written by local newspapers or special interest groups. This approach discourages "borrowing" material written by others.

The first part of the analysis deals with the audience of persuasion. Since persuasive messages are created with the goal of influencing members of a target audience, the analysis should state who the specific audience is and why they were chosen. This analysis centers both on the demographics and "psychographics" of the audience. Information concerning the age, gender, educational, socio-economic, political, and ethnic and/or racial make-up of the target group is coupled with a determination of the group's values, beliefs, attitudes, and opinions on the subject of the message.

Second, since target audience members are, in part, influenced by emotional appeals, the analysis should focus on the motivators employed—those forces that stimulate or direct one's attitude or behavior—and why they were chosen, given the topic and the target audience. I introduce my students to a variety of motivators, such as fear, anger, sympathy, independence, ethnicity, devotion, and nostalgia, before giving the assignment. The analysis of motivators indicates how well the appeals fit the audience's needs, wants, and desires.

Third, since the manner in which a message is expressed has an effect on the audience, an analysis of language choices is required. Certain words or phrases may have been chosen, due to their ability to name things, connect thoughts, or spark an emotion. Other words or phrases are chosen for the meaning they carry. For example, in a message on hunting, the word *harvest* carries a very different meaning than *kill*, when used to describe what hunters do. Still other words or phrases may help to create mood, as when a beer manufacturer urges consumers to "Capture Canada's Bear of Beers," suggesting a mood of manly ruggedness and adventure.

Fourth, since some type of evidence usually is necessary to influence members of a target audience, the analysis centers on what approach has been taken. Persuaders may use evidence that appeals to the intellect of the audience. This *rational* approach to evidence employs facts, statistics, or other data that stand independent of the individual employing them. Persuaders may use evidence that appeals to the audience's emotions. This *dramatic* approach to evidence employs anecdotes and illustrations which provide characterization and setting, "forcing" audiences vicariously to experience the evidence. Yet another possibility is using a combination of both of these approaches to appeal to the "whole person."

Finally, since the manner in which arguments, evidence, and appeals to emotions are ordered has an effect on audiences, an analysis of the chosen organizational pattern is required. Students may employ a causal, topical, spatial, chronological, stock issues, or motivated sequence pattern, but it is important they understand that the choice is constrained by both the subject and the audience.

Student reaction to these analyses has been very positive for several reasons. They enable students to put into practice the theories of persuasion studied throughout the semester. They enhance students' ability to make meaningful choices among a variety of possible persuasive approaches. Moreover, since the persuasive message is presented in class, peers as well as the instructor have an opportunity to evaluate the message and the tactics employed. This allows for a thorough discussion of the strengths and weaknesses, the effectiveness and ineffectiveness of tactical persuasive choices.

Howard N. Schreier

Speech Anxiety

Coping With Speech Anxiety

Goal: To help students cope with speech anxiety.

Speech anxiety is a perennial problem. Everyone who teaches public speaking knows that the major obstacle many beginning speakers encounter is speech anxiety.

The following activities are designed to help students cope with speech anxiety. These activities can be conducted with an entire class, but our experience indicates that students who are not speech anxious become impatient with this unit. We suggest offering the unit as a voluntary out-of-class workshop. Enrollment should be limited to 15 students per workshop. J. Ady's M.A. thesis, *Testing a Workshop to Reduce Public Speaking Anxiety...* (Washington State University, 1987) indicates this type of workshop effectively reduces speech anxiety.

The workshop is presented in the following manner.

Introduction

Students receive an overview of the workshop elements.

General Speaking Anxiety

Students receive training in systematic densensitization (SD) to cope with general speech anxiety. They learn about J. Wolpe's rationale for SD in *Psychotherapy by Reciprocal Inhibition*, Stanford University Press, 1958)—i.e. since one cannot be fearful and relaxed at the same time, if one can learn to relax in feared circumstances, one will no longer feel fearful. At this point, students learn deep muscle relaxation. James McCroskey's *Deep Muscular Relaxation Tape with Accompanying Hierarchies of Anxiety Stimuli for 7th Grade, 10th Grade, and College Level Students*, #801, may be purchased for $6.00 from the Speech Communication Association's national office to use in this portion of the workshop. Students progress through a fear hierarchy—beginning with the least feared speaking situations and ending with the most feared speaking situations. Several speech fear hierarchies are in print including G.L. Paul's *Insight vs. Desensitization in Psychotherapy: An Experiment in Anxiety Reduction* (Stanford, CA: Stanford University Press, 1958) and J. Deffenbacher's "Hierarchies for Desensitization of Test and Speech Anxieties," in the *Journal of College Student Personnel*, 15 (1974), 453. You also may construct your own hierarchy by asking each student to identify ten speaking situations that range from the least to the most feared situations.

While the students are listening to the systematic desensitization tape, the instructor compiles a representative hierarchy from their lists. Students, whose eyes remain closed, are asked to imagine a public speaking scene while remaining relaxed. If someone feels anxious while imagining a scene, s/he raises one finger. When anyone indicates feeling anxious, the entire group is told to stop thinking about the scene and to relax (by doing muscle relaxation exercises, if necessary). When everyone appears relaxed, we ask them to imagine the same scene again. Repeat this process until everyone can imagine every scene without feeling anxious.

Specific Speech Anxiety

While systematic desensitization is useful for general speech anxiety, anxiety can arise due to the unique nature of a specific speech. To help students cope with specific speech anxiety, we cover the following tactics that may be used at different stages in a speech.

Immediately before the speech: repeat the goal and main points of the speech to yourself; go over the introduction to the speech; check note cards to make sure they are in the correct order; and think about stories (anecdotes, examples, etc.) to use if anxiety becomes intense.

In the introduction to the speech: use something that you know well for the introduction (i.e., don't do novel, risky things); use a visual aid to focus attention away from you (visual aids also are useful mnemonic devices); have good notes but don't read directly from these notes (if you avoid looking at the audience, it will only be harder to look at them later).

In the body of the speech: use visual aids that contain vital information in order to overcome possible lapses of memory; have good notes in good order; concentrate on your ideas; by all means—know your material!

In the conclusion of the speech: use time-worn techniques (summary, a familiar story, etc.).

In the question/answer period after the speech: anticipate questions; avoid defensiveness—recognize the worth of the other person and focus on ideas; repeat the question so you will understand it and will have time to plan a response; if you don't know the answer, just say so.

Space prohibits detailed development of the rationale behind each of these items but the rationale for several of these items may be found in W.W. Brownell and R.A. Katula's "The Communication Anxiety Graph: A Classroom Tool for Managing Speech Anxiety," in *Communication Quarterly* (1984), 32, 243-249.

Speech Delivery

Students receive a speech topic and deliver a 1-2 minute speech. During the preparation time allowed for this presentation, the speaker is encouraged to use the tactics we pointed out in the previous activities to cope with any anxiety that arises. Just prior to delivering this speech, students experience visualization—a procedure designed to encourage positive thinking. (See J. Ayres and T.S. Hopf, "Visualization: A Means of Reducing Speech Anxiety," *Communication Education, 34, 318-323.)* The visualization script we use follows:

Close your eyes and allow your body to get comfortable in the chair in which you are sitting. Move around until you are in a position that will continue to be relaxing for you for the next ten to fifteen minutes. Take a deep, comfortable breath and hold it...now slowly release it through your nose (if possible). That is right. . . now take another deep breath and make certain that you are breathing from the diaphragm (from your belly). . . hold it. . . and now release it slowly. . . and begin your normal breathing pattern. (Shift around if you need to get comfortable again.)

I now want you to begin to visualize the beginning of this presentation. See yourself full of energy, full of confidence, looking forward to the speech. You feel thoroughly prepared for the task at hand. The audience appears quite friendly and supportive. You feel ABSOLUTELY sure of your material and your ability to present the information in a forceful, convincing, positive manner. You are feeling very good about this presentation and see yourself move forward eagerly to make the presentation when your name is called. All of your material is well organized and well planned.

Now you see yourself presenting your talk. It is really quite brilliant (if I do say so myself) and has all the fitness of a polished, professional speaker. You also are aware that your audience is giving you head nods, smiles, and other positive responses that clearly give you the message that you are truly "on target." You conclude with a clinching summary. You now see yourself fielding audience questions with confidence and energy. You see yourself receiving the congratulations of your classmates. You are relaxed, pleased with your talk, and ready for the next task, filled with energy, purpose, and a sense of general well-being. Congratulate yourself on a job well done!

Now. . . I want you to begin to return to this time and place. Take a deep breath. . . hold it. . . and let it go. Do this several times and move slowly back into the room. Take as much time as you need. . .

The student then presents the speech and others are asked to comment. The comments about the presentation are constructive and focus on how the anxiety reduction techniques were used.

Joe Ayres, Theodore S. Hopf, and Jeff Ady

A Course On Stage Fright

Goal: To help students manage their stage fright.

The greatest fear Americans experience next to fear of dying is the fear of public speaking.

For the past two years I have taught a workshop at the University of Missouri-Kansas City in controlling stage fright. Below are some of the ideas I shared with the students, followed by some assignments used in the workshop.

The course is called controlling the fear of public speaking, rather than conquering that fear, because you never really eliminate stage fright nor should you. Naomi Graffman writes in *Horizon*, September, 1981, "Stage fright is the result of the 'fight or flight' syndrome." In other words, stage fright is the result of a sudden shot of adrenalin that enables one to be able to meet the challenge of difficult situations. This is the same kind of charge experienced by athletes and musicians that causes them to be at their best, at the "cutting edge" of their ability.

Five suggestions for controlling speech tensions are in the form of the five "p's" for easy remembering. They are: *pick* a familiar subject on which to speak, *practice* frequently, *picture* the audience as friends, *position* oneself to be free from tension, and *pace* the rate of speaking more slowly than in previous speech experiences.

One of the best ways to control stage fright is to *pick* a familiar subject on which to speak. The subject that most interests the students will always be the one with which he or she is familiar. Encourage students to brainstorm on those topics they know best in an initial preparation session. They might try presenting short impromptu speeches on their two or three favorite topics to detect which is most effective. Speaking on a subject one likes will not only be more relaxing, but it is easier to locate supporting materials on a topic which is both familiar and enjoyable. An added dividend is that the audience will be more apt to be interested in the subject which the speaker finds interesting.

Practice develops confidence. Once the student has prepared a phrase outline, he or she should practice twenty or thirty minutes, six or seven times over a four-to-five day period. Be sure to caution students to practice aloud standing as if delivering the speech to the audience. If possible, at least one of the practice sessions should be in the room where the speech is to be delivered. Even if one is going to make a challenging proposal from the floor at a meeting, it will build confidence to attempt a trial run in the room where the student will do this.

Urge students to be a friend to the audience and *picture* them as friends. The audience members want every speaker to succeed. Every major text on speech advises the speaker to pay attention to feedback from the audience in the form of laughter, applause, intense silence, and facial expression. The speaker should use expressions of interest to bolster self-confidence.

How can one be free from tension? The speaker needs to assume a *position* in which tension is less apt to develop. One physical manifestation of too much adrenalin is a tendency to stiffen limbs. If the speaker can remain in the hall outside the room where the speech is to be delivered, some stretching exercises to unwind will be helpful. If the speaker is sitting in full view of an audience, he or she can still relax arms and legs as well as take a few easy breaths.

Finally, if tension occurs while delivering the talk, the speaker should *pace* the speech more slowly. When adrenalin shoots through our systems, we tense our inner vocal folds which create a higher pitch as they are tightened. As the pitch goes up, timing accelerates and volume increases. Conversely, if a speaker purposefully reduces the rate of speaking, the other vocal characteristics tend to become more relaxed. Michael Motley in "Taking the Terror out of Talk," *Psychology Today*, January 1988, also reminds us that a slower rate benefits the audience. "People in an audience," writes Motley, "have a tremendous job of information-processing to do. They need your help. Slow down, pause and guide the audience through your talk by delineating major and minor points carefully."

One doesn't learn how to swim, type, or play a musical instrument without doing it. Students should be taught to welcome speaking opportunities. The student should start by asking for invitations to speak before small groups. Speaking more frequently during meetings at one's place of employment is a good way to start.

During the course of the workshop I ask the students to role-play situations that are fear-producing in real life such as job interviews, introducing celebrities, visiting with supervisors, and negotiating an argument between two upset people.

A speech communication class should deal with life situations. The approaches described above may be used with students particularly ill-at-ease in a speech fundamentals course, as well as in a public-address class dealing with stage fright.

Harry Langdon

Speech Assignments—General

A Speech About A "Great American Speech"

Goal: To help students understand public speech as a complex rhetorical event (with historical, social, biographical, and linguistic elements).

This assignment helps students develop basic library/research skills while applying basic rhetorical standards (organization, content, development, and audience analysis) to the analysis of a significant rhetorical event in American history. It also helps them to acquire knowledge of the history of public address, rhetorical criticism, and organizational skills as they prepare their own speech.

Distribute a list of possible speakers/speeches from which, each student will select a speaker no one else has chosen. The list should include historical figures such as Patrick Henry (Give Me Liberty), Jonathan Edwards, Stephen Douglas, Abraham Lincoln, Elizabeth Cady Stanton, Mary Baker Eddy, Theodore Roosevelt (Muckrakers), Woodrow Wilson, F.D. Roosevelt, John F. Kennedy, Martin Luther King, Jr., Richard Nixon (Checkers), Barbara Jordan, and Ronald Reagan.

You may check your library to be sure information on each speaker is available. The most valuable resources, such as Brigance and Hochmuth's three volume set, *History and Criticism of American Public Address* or Duffy and Ryan's *American Orators of the Twentieth Century,* should be placed on library reserve.

Students will prepare a 10-12 minute speech which describes/analyzes significant aspects of the speech event. A sample outline format might look like this:

I. Occasion
  A. Historical setting
  B. Particular purpose for the speech
II. Speaker
  A. Training as a speaker
  B. Pertinent philosophical/political/religious orientations
  C. Delivery style
III. Content Analysis
  A. Purpose/thesis
  B. Organization/support
  C. Stylistic devices
IV. Audience Effect
  A. Immediate
  B. Historical

Students may be critiqued according to standards for: *content* (Did the speech adequately clarify, organize, and analyze the speech event according to the outline?); *delivery* (Did the speaker speak fluently, with adequate volume, expressive modulation, and clear articulation?); and *style* (Did the speaker use language, stylistic devices, and images oriented to the audience?)

Barbara Adler

Creating an Extra and "Real Life" Public Speaking Assignment

Goal: To add one brief "real life" speaking assignment that will have a built-in attention-getting element, and that will take a minimum of class time.

Anyone who attends typical club meetings, church services and other public gatherings knows that *the most frequently given speeches* are always announcements, informing the members of a coming event and encouraging them to attend or take part in it. Their customary position early in the meeting, and before any

formal program, insures some inherent audience attention and this encourages speakers to be imaginative in phrasing the basic facts and appeals for participation in a very brief presentation.

The natural time for such a speech in the classroom is at the very beginning of the period, with the speaker introduced by the teacher or whoever is presiding, or simply invited by asking, "Are there any announcements today?"

The speaking dates can be determined by circulating a "sign up" sheet on the first day of the class and specifying that (if possible) no more than one announcement be scheduled for each day. The student should be free to select any event he or she wishes as the subject. It can be a sports event, a school social activity, a club meeting, a day to be commemorated, a public lecture or play or movie, or any other significant event. (One student used the latter category by "announcing" her engagement to be married!) The only two rules are (1) that the event be real, and (2) that the speech be no longer than 3 minutes (or about 400 words, or 2 double-spaced typed pages).

Advantages: (1) The announcement speech may be evaluated as any other oral assignment (clarity of information, style of phrasing, effectiveness of presentation, etc.). (2) Because of its brevity, it can be slipped into the daily schedule and each student will have performed a common assignment over the term without allocating several whole class periods to it. (3) It will be a "real life" application of public speaking skills.

J. Jeffrey Auer

Extemporizing Through Humor and Repetition

Goal: To use extemporaneous speeches to help students develop speaking skills and to confront the common problem of overcoming fear and lack of confidence faced by first-time speakers.

The well known entertainer, the late George Jessel said, "The human brain is a wonderful thing. It starts working the moment we are born and never stops until you stand up to speak in public." Most speakers, especially first-time speakers, can relate to the experiences of the cotton mouth, sweaty palms, and the brain dysfunction which often occur when standing before a group of people to speak. However, frequently during our lives we are asked to "get up and think on our feet" as we say a few words, or extemporize. I use two exercises to help students to:

1. Organize information and ideas logically.
2. Analyze questions and topics.
3. Communicate effectively.
4. Develop critical listening skills.

The first exercise is a warm-up exercise to reduce fear which I call Truth or Lie. It requires students to speak without preparation in a supportive classroom environment. It allows students to get to know one another, using humor and is a preparation for timed speeches.

Before class, students are asked to bring an object which will fit in a brown lunch bag. At the beginning of class, the objects are dropped (with secrecy) into a container. Students are cautioned not to share their object's identity with classmates.

Truth or Lie is delivered panel style. Students are asked to number off, one to three. Students with the same number serve on the same panel. One of the panels quickly goes to the front of the room and meets privately with the instructor. Members share the identity of their objects. The instructor selects one object, such as a golf ball, and its owner is acknowledged by the panel. The object is placed secretly in the paper bag in front of the class.

The panel begins individual descriptions of what's in the bag. Panel members follow two rules. First, the owner of the golf ball is bound to tell the truth when rendering his/her description of the object. Second, the remaining panel members are encouraged to be "creative" with their descriptions of the object. Lies and gross exaggerations are acceptable fare. A miniature godzilla may lurk in the bag, according to these students. Each panel member is allowed a 1-minute presentation.

The class votes on which panel member is telling the truth and the panel receiving the most wrong guesses wins the event. Then a new object is selected and the process resumes. Not more than 15 minutes should be allowed for the entire game. Usually, 2-3 class periods are needed to involve the entire class in this game.

The second exercise is Round-Robin. Students begin by keeping the numbers they had in the previous exercise. The instructor distributes an instruction sheet which indicates the students have 5 minutes to *write* a 2 minute extemporaneous speech on one of the following:

The thing I value most in life is:
The hardest thing I have ever had to do was:
The funniest experience I have ever had was:
Some people bother me because of their:
The most frightening experience I have ever had was:
I feel strongly that:
Or
Tell of an incident when you had to ask for help.
Tell about your most embarrassing moment.
Tell about something you wanted very badly and finally got or didn't get.
Describe an incident in your life which you feel may shown you might have ESP.
Describe your greatest triumph or defeat.
Describe an experience with another person which moved you deeply.

The information sheet also indicates the class will divide into 3 groups and that students will present their speeches to each group, every 2 minutes or so. The procedure is further explained as follows:

1. The first time you speak, you will sit and you may use your note cards. Attempt to familiarize yourself with the ideas.

2. The second time you speak, you will sit but use fewer notes. Force yourself to depend more on developing ideas as you speak (extemporize)—.

3. The third time you speak, you may not use notes and you must stand. Concentrate on full communication.

Students form groups consisting of a 1, 2, and 3 in each group. Then, students #1 in each group deliver their prepared speeches within the group. The teacher calls "time" after about 2 minutes and students #1 in each group move clockwise to the next nearest group. The process begins again and continues until the teacher calls "time." Students #1 shift one more time and present the speech to the third group. The speaking round-robin next requires students #2 in each group to continue the process. Finally, students #3 take their turns at speaking.

For evaluation purposes, at the end of the unit, each student is required to deliver a 2-3 minute extemporaneous speech in front of the entire class.

Rhonda Ehrler

The Heckling Speech

Goal: To provide a speaking situation that will afford students an opportunity to practice immediate adaptation to audience feedback.

In this country, speakers and listeners have been conditioned to repress their reactions to one another during a public address. Heckling usually is considered impolite. However, I have found that, within the controlled environment of my advanced public speaking course, the heckling speech is an excellent exercise for teaching speakers to successfully confront a questioning audience. The threat of heckling forces speakers to choose ideas and words carefully and to be thoroughly knowledgeable with their subjects.

The main objectives of this activity are to teach students to:

1. Apply knowledge during a speech.
2. Contend with negative public comments.
3. Understand the nature and scope of messages of dissent.
4. Think and edit on one's feet.
5. Treat questions with respect.
6. State and defend a personal value.

After discussing the nature of the rhetoric of dissent, I assign a 3-7 minute persuasive speech in which students must argue for a policy change through a status quo mechanism. (Usually subjects range anywhere from banning sex from television ads to the continued legalization of all terrain vehicles.) Students are required to speak from a brief outline. Also, they are required to submit an extensive, complete sentence outline (which includes documentation) to me before they

begin their presentations. During the speech, a 3 minute "heckling period" occurs between the 2 and 5 minute marks.

The regulations and format for governing the heckling period are as follows:

1. Each student selects a chairperson to sit at the front of the class and properly acknowledge every heckler's request to speak, thus avoiding chaos.

2. At the 2 minute mark, a timekeeper waves a "begin" sign and, conversely, a "stop" sign at the 5 minute mark. All audience comments must cease at that point. Speakers use the final 2 minutes to edit and conclude their remarks.

3. During the heckling period, a member of the audience may interrupt the speaker by raising a hand and calling, "Mr./Miss Chairman/woman." After being properly recognized, the heckler is permitted to ask a question or make a comment.

4. Speakers must respectfully respond to each question or comment. They must maintain their composure and are never allowed to retaliate with a sarcastic remark or the use of "put down" humor.

5. Speakers may be subject *only* to verbal harrassment.

I have been using the heckling speech for 18 years. Initially, students greet the exercise with apprehension, followed by a steel-willed determination to contend with the heckling experience successfully. Afterwards, they feel proud of the accomplishment and note the benefits of the activity. Such comments as, "I learned to maintain my self-control in spite of a hostile group of listeners" are common. Also, I have observed that this activity always creates or increases fraternal feelings of acceptance, support, tolerance, and objectivity within the group. Finally, this activity provides an opportunity for students to contend with a real speaking threat successfully, without having to confront agonizing consequences.

C. Darrell Langley

Practical Ceremonial Speaking: Three Speech Activities

Goal: To provide students with practical speaking experience in 3 common ceremonial situations: introducing a speaker, announcing an award, and accepting an award.

Ceremonial speaking is one of the most common uses of public speaking skills for Americans. Speech students will be called upon to make ceremonial speeches, both prepared and impromptu, in many social and business contexts. Many students currently are involved in organizations that require pubic speaking, and certainly they will be faced with this opportunity in the future. Speech teachers can provide students with the training necessary in both content and delivery, of ceremonial speeches that will be effective and interesting.

As a supplement to the common informative and persuasive speeches in a public speaking course, I use 3 common ceremonial speaking situations that students find entertaining as well as educational. I review the elements that students may include in each speech in an assignment sheet, and I encourage students to show sincerity and originality in selecting the topics for their speeches. The more that they express sincere feelings and concern for the topic, the more interesting the assignment will be.

Assignment 1: Introducing a Speaker. Imagine that you could invite any famous living or deceased person to your class to give a 30-minute speech. Whom would you select? Your task is to give a 3-minute speech of introduction that will motivate the audience to listen to this speaker. For nationally famous people who are living, you may wish to Consult *Who's Who in America*. For historical personages, consult the *Dictionary of American Biography*. Elements you may wish to include in your introduction include the following:

- biographical data about the person,
- important contributions made by the person,
- relevance of the speaker for this audience,
- the topic the speaker will address,
- why the speaker is important to you.

Assignment 2: The Award Speech. Towards the end of your class term, select a classmate to whom you wish to give an award. Prepare a 5-minute award presentation speech. The award may be for some positive personality trait, such as "Most Optimistic Person" or "Best Sense of Humor." It also may emphasize some skill or ability, such as "Best Use of Visual Aids" or "Best Racquetball Player." The award might also be entirely fanciful, such as "Best Person with Whom to Go to the Moon" or "Person with the Brightest Future." Be positive and sincere in your remarks. Elements you may wish to include in the speech are:

- the nature and history of the award (invent one if necessary),
- praise for the audience or organization presenting the award,
- the special characteristics of the recipient,
- specific examples of the recipient's meritorious behavior,
- the impact and importance of the recipient's behavior,
- inspiration to follow the recipient's example.

Assignment 3: Accepting the Award. Once you have received an award in Assignment 2, immediately make a 2-minute impromptu speech of acceptance. Elements you may wish to include in your acceptance speech include the following:

- thanks to the person or group providing the award,
- thanks to everyone involved in the awards process,
- praise for people who have helped you in your success,
- the meaningfulness of the award to you,
- the positive values in your achievement,
- any personal message you might have for the audience.

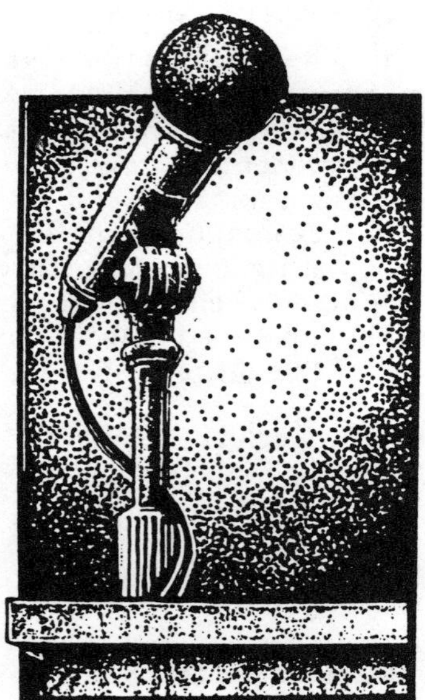

These ceremonial speeches evoke a tremendous amount of excitement in the classroom. The speaking situations become very realistic, and students are motivated to high levels of eloquence, wit, and sincerity. Instructors can use this high level of enthusiasm as a solid basis on which to make teaching points regarding audience analysis, appropriateness of language, and originality of invention.

Randall E. Majors

The Challenging Audience Exercise

Goal: To help advanced public speaking students apply theories about hostile audiences and attitude modification to their research, construction, presentation, and evaluation of "challenging audience" speeches.

Business and other professional presentations rarely proceed without interrupting questions — and at times, strenuous objections. This class activity is designed to prepare students for the "challenging audience." The activity has a two-fold purpose: 1. to encourage students to develop persuasive strategies that deal specifically with the disagreeing audience and, 2. to help students build confidence in responding to audience questions.

First, compile a list of controversial topics (with a few left blank to be suggested by students). A straw poll is taken of the class. When there is a ⅔ majority for or against a particular issue, that topic becomes eligible for selection by the student. Of course, the student will take the minority point of view. The "Sample of Audience Topic List" could contain the list of topics at the left, listed under "Are you in favor of:" and two columns at the right under the headings "Yes" and "No." Some of the topics might be: birth control ads on TV; banning beer and wine ads on TV; lethal injections for capital punishment; televised trials; smokers' rights; mandatory service in the military; six-year presidential term; parents teaching children at home; X-rated cable TV; Jesse Helms; state lotteries; squeal ruling for minors and birth control; midwives; the tenure system; labelling music G, PG, R, or X-rated; Edwin Meese; beauty pageants; revising grand jury system; chiropractory being recognized by the AMA; and drug testing of employees.

A week or more before the hostile audience speech is due, the class has a "survey day." Students discover the specific attitudes about their topics by creating and administering a simple written survey using a Likert Scale (Strongly Agree, Agree, Undecided, Disagree, Strongly Disagree) for each item. For example, the following questions might be on the survey for a speech dealing with nuclear weapons.

1. I am well informed about the US nuclear weapons testing program.
2. The US must maintain a strong nuclear weapons arsenal.
3. Underground testing of nuclear weapons presents a serious environmental harm.
4. Developing new nuclear weapons decreases the possibility that war will occur.
5. US nuclear weapons testing should be expanded.
6. The US should strive to eliminate ALL nuclear weapons in existence.

Students may phrase some of their questions for and against the topic to create a sounder survey. Based on the audience survey, students can begin constructing their speeches to adapt to the specific knowledge, needs, and fears of the listeners. The speech is twelve to fifteen minutes long with a two-minute uninterrupted summary allowed at the end. (Time constraints will depend on class size.)

To motivate students to begin asking questions or stating objections, assign three students to speak up during each speech. Usually, after the first day, students get into the "spirit" and assigning "hecklers" no longer is necessary.

Immediately, at the end of the speech, a post-speech survey is passed out (identical to the pre-speech survey) to determine how much, if any, attitude change occured. A three-page paper then is written by the student discussing four major points. 1. How successful was the speech? 2. What suggestions were made by the instructor and student? 3. What were the strengths and weaknesses of the speech? 4. If the speech were given again, what would you, as the speaker, do differently and why? The purpose of the paper is to determine how much the student learned about audience analysis, strategies of persuasion, fielding questions, and audience oriented communication in general.

Students consistently have stated that this speech was the most beneficial of the required speeches of the semester. The Challenging Audience speech works particularly well after units on attitude theory and change, hostile audiences, and speaker responses to questions and objections. (I am indebted to Dr. Bill Hill, Assistant Professor of Speech Communication at UNCC for handouts which were used in developing the Challenging Audience Paper and the "Survey Questionnaire.") This speech is not recommended for most introductory public speaking courses.

Charlynn Ross

The Speech To Explain Difficult Ideas

Goal: To provide students with research-based strategies for explaining difficult ideas and practice in explanatory speaking.

In this era, information may be easy to obtain but good explanations are rare. Everyone appreciates an excellent explanation of how microchips work or why the AIDS virus cannot be transmitted through swimming pools, but we also know that good explanations and good explainers are scarce.

An ideal way to teach strategies for effective explaining is to assign the "speech to explain difficult ideas." In this report, I summarize research on good explaining and describe the procedures I use to teach explanatory speaking. A unit on explaining works well in introductory, technical, or business speaking classes.

Definition. The speech to explain is a type of informative presentation. Informative speeches primarily create awareness or understanding, whereas explanatory speeches chiefly create understanding. For example, a speech on how to fax a document creates awareness, whereas a speech on how fax machines work deepens understanding.

Topics for explanatory speeches come from constantly asking "why" or "what does that mean?" Some of my favorites: Why do people yawn? What are modern artists trying to achieve? Why are water towers shaped like giant mushrooms? How does nuclear fusion work? Why is irradiated food healthful? What does "evolution" mean? What's a municipal bond?

According to research, there are at least three ways in which answers to these and similar questions may be difficult for lay audiences to understand (for a review of this research, see Katherine E. Rowan, "A Contemporary Theory of Explanatory Writing." *Written Communication*, 5 (1988): 23-56). These include difficulties in (a) understanding the meaning and use of a term, (b) abstracting the main points from complex information, and (c) grasping an implausible or counter-intuitive proposition (such as Einstein's notion that we are accelerating toward the center of the Earth). The challenge for explanatory speakers is diagnosing the principal difficulty facing their audience and shaping their speech to overcome that difficulty.

Types of difficulties and explanations. If the audience's chief difficulty rests with understanding the meaning and use of a certain term, then speakers should develop speeches providing *elucidating explanations.* Elucidating explanations illuminate a concept's meaning and use. For example, speakers principally concerned with explaining concepts such as "evolution" and "municipal bond" should use elucidating explanations.

According to research (Merrill and Tennyson's *Teaching Concepts*, Englewood Cliffs, NJ: Educational Technology Publications, 1977) good elucidating explanations contain: (a) a definition that lists each of the concept's critical features, (b) an array of varied examples and nonexamples (nonexamples are instances that audiences often think are examples but are not), and (c) opportunities for audiences to distinguish examples from nonexamples by looking for the concept's critical features.

One particularly effective elucidating speech explained what "science" means. The student began:

> We all know what science is. It's what Carl Sagan and Mr. Wizard do, right? Since we know, we should agree on some basic ideas. How many people think biology is a science? (Nearly all hands rise.) How many think psychology is? (A few hands rise.) How about astrology? (A few hands rise.)

This speech was effective because, after establishing that "science" is hard to explain, the speaker offered a definition listing the concept's critical features, gave an array of examples and nonexamples of science (e.g., psychology vs. astrology), and offered the audience opportunities to distinguish examples from nonexamples with a short oral quiz.

If an idea is difficult chiefly because its complexity obscures its main points or the "big picture," then speakers should present a *quasi-scientific explanation.* Just as scientists try to develop models of the world, quasi-scientific explanations model or picture the key dimensions of some phenomenon for lay audiences. Speakers presenting complex topics to laypersons—topics such as how microchips work, the similarities and differences between Buddhism and Christianity, or how DNA molecules pass along genetic information—should use quasi-scientific explanations.

According to research, effective quasi-scientific explanations contain features that highlight the main points of the explanation, features such as titles, organizing analogies, visual aids, and signalling phrases (e.g., "The first key point is"). Good quasi-scientific explanations also contain features that *connect* key points, such as transitional phrases ("for example"), connectives ("because"), and diagrams depicting relationships among parts.

For example, a particularly good quasi-scientific speech explained how radar works. Using an organizing analogy, the speaker said that radar works essentially the way an echo does, except that radio waves, rather than sound waves, are sent and received. The presentation was effective because consistent references to this analogy highlighted its main points.

If the chief source of difficulty is not a particular term, nor a complex mass of information, but rather the counter-intuitivity of the idea itself, then speakers should design their talks as *transformative explanations.* For example, the idea that when people push on a concrete wall, that wall exerts an equal and opposite force on them (Newton's Third Law of Motion) contains no difficult terms and little detail, but, from a lay perspective, it just seems impossible. Transformative explanations are designed to present such counter-intuitive ideas by helping lay audiences transform their everyday "theories" of phenomena into more accepted notions. Questions best answered with transformative explanations might include: why we are accelerating toward the Earth's center, why irradiated food is healthful, or why perception is a subjective process.

According to research, transformative explanations are most effective when they: (a) state people's "implicit" or "lay" theory about the phenomenon; (b) acknowledge the apparent plausibility of this lay theory; (c) demonstrate its inadequacy; (d) state the more accepted account, and (e) demonstrate its greater adequacy.

Speech communication teachers often give good transformative explanations when they lecture on the notion that perception is a subjective, rather than an objective, process. As instructors, we know that simply asserting perception's subjectivity would not be effective. Consequently, we usually begin our lectures by acknowledging the apparent plausibility of the "objective-perception hypothesis." That is, we tell our students that it's natural to assume that what they perceive is exactly correspondent to reality. But then we demonstrate the inadequacy of the objective-perception hypothesis by using optical illusions or attribution exercises, showing that the mind partly creates the reality it perceives. Only after these exercises, do we explain the subjectivity of perception.

I have found that explanatory speech rounds are some of my favorites. Students try challenging topics and are impressed with how difficult it is to explain ideas well. Some have discovered that the strategies they learn for good explaining can also work as study tips. In this information era, it's good for us to slow down and thoroughly understand small but important bits of information. Explanatory speaking is a step in that direction.

Katherine Rowan

Custom Comparison Speeches

Goal: To have students learn about their own cultures and to encourage a broadening of non-biased cultural perspectives.

So often, with customs and traditions, even of one's own culture, the reasons for them are unknown. We celebrate events in a certain manner simply because they have been a part of our socialization process. Take, for example, the sending of Christmas cards, first-time brides in the U.S. wearing white, or the wrapping of presents. People are often at a loss for an explanation of such practices.

The basic idea of custom comparison speeches is to have students deliver a speech to inform on a specific custom or tradition of their culture by exploring it and comparing it to a parallel custom or tradition of another culture. Students select and research a custom to find out how it came about, what particular things are done on the occasion, and why. The speeches should include the significance and meaning behind the rituals associated with their custom or tradition.

This assignment is rich as a learning experience because:

1. Students are exposed to new ideas. As they find out about other cultures, they may begin to question how values and ideas are passed on.
2. Students not only go to the library to accomplish the research aspect of the assignment, but many speak with parents and grandparents to gather information.
3. Students see a variety of practices as reasonable and thus are less likely to judge things which are different as right or wrong.

A variation on the assignment is to use an ESL class as partners for your speech students. Students can work in pairs and compare a related custom from their two cultures.

The assignment of custom comparison speeches is an interesting, enjoyable, and enriching experience. It can help students move toward a broadening of non-biased cultural perspectives which should be a growing concern of today's academic communities.

Allison Schumer

Speech Assignments—Impromptu Speeches

Using Quotations As Impromptu Speech Topics

Goal: To provide students with the opportunity to demonstrate both their knowledge of course concepts and their impromptu speaking skills.

"How can I speak about a topic that I don't know anything about?" is a frequent complaint of students in my basic public speaking class. While I usually rebuff their criticisms with a cajoling, "Of course, you do. Just think about it" or a sarcastic, "Where have you been for the last 20 years," part of me (as a past student and now as a teacher who has listened to a few years of impromptu speaking based on the pick-a-topic-out-of-the-hat approach) feels that their comments have validity. I incorporate impromptu speaking into the class because it forces students to think on their feet. Unfortunately, some students do not have a broad base of knowledge on current issues. Consequently, many of their impromptu speeches are ineffective because they are laden with generalities and repetition, rather than supported with concrete details, examples, and so on. In other words, while speeches have structure, they have little substance.

With knowledge comes substance, so I designed an impromptu speech that capitilizes on something that I know students have knowledge of—their public speaking course. From various chapter headings of assorted communication texts and from reference books such as *Familiar Quotations*, I collected 40 or so quotations on public speaking or communication-related topics. These quotations vary from the comical, "Reading a speech is like kissing through a veil," to the more serious "Speak that I may see you" (Socrates).

To make the quotations easy to read, I type them, all capital letters and double-spaced, on 5" x 8" index cards. Students draw 2 cards out of "a hat" and then select one to develop into a 2-3 minute impromptu speech. To prepare students for their speech, I suggest that they do the following:

1. Determine what studied concept or point is expressed by the quotation. For example, "Reading a speech is like kissing through a veil" relates to delivery.
2. Decide where to place the quotation. That is, would it be more effective in the introduction or in the conclusion?
3. Concentrate on supporting their interpretation by drawing on information gained from lectures, discussions, readings, and from listening to past speeches.

I am pleased by the quality of the speeches given. When polled for their reactions, most students felt confident with their own presentations and impressed with what they heard. While this speech may be given at almost any time during the semester, it is especially useful at the end—for impromptu presentations given during the last class serve a dual purpose: I gather how much students have absorbed and the speeches serve as a course summary, leaving me to provide only a final commentary.

Kathleen Beauchene

The "Just a Minute" Impromptu Exercise

Goal: To increase the ability of public speaking students to use language effectively.

The British conduct civilized quiz shows, with an emphasis more on wit and cleverness than one finds on "Wheel of Fortune." A year ago I was listening to such a show, "Just a Minute," on the World Service of the BBC and I adopted the idea for use as an impromptu exercise in public speaking. Students like it (one student even reported playing it with her family on a long car trip), but even better, speaking improves as a result of playing it.

The rules are straightforward. Four contestants are in turn given a common word to speak on for 60 seconds (i.e., donut, piano, elephant). However, the speaker can be challenged for one of three reasons by the three other contestants:

1. Hesitation, including nonfluencies
2. Deviation from the topic or from the rules of grammar
3. Repetition of words unnecessarily. (This is the hardest rule. The topic can be repeated, as can pronouns, articles and prepositions, and perhaps the verb "to be." But nouns, verbs, adjectives, and adverbs may not be repeated.)

When a contestant thinks the speaker has violated a rule, he or she yells out a challenge, which is adjudicated by the instructor. A successful challenger receives one point and the opportunity to continue speaking for whatever is left of the original minute. A player who makes a successful challenge at the 55 second point has five seconds left to continue on the topic (a stopwatch is needed). A speaker who is incorrectly challenged receives a point and may continue speaking.

The person who is speaking at the conclusion of the minute receives a point. In the rare case that a person speaks the full minute without being challenged, he or she receives two points. With advanced students, additional points may be awarded for particularly clever, absurd challenges (as is the practice on the BBC).

A round consists of each of the four contestants receiving a word and takes six to ten minutes of class time. In a class of 20, I typically have a final round consisting of the winners of the preliminary rounds.

The exercise helps to make students aware of nonfluencies (i.e., "um" and "uh"), and unnecessary words (i.e., "you know," "sorta," "kinda"). It reminds them that variation in vocabulary is useful, and it refreshes some as to standard grammar. Students report being more sensitive to these matters after a round of "Just a Minute."

The exercise keeps all involved. I find that even those who are not currently contestants, follow the four speakers avidly, wincing when an egregious failing goes unchallenged.

I use a lot of impromptu exercises; this one has quickly become a favorite.

Randall Bytwerk

International Bazaar

Goal: To improve students' research and listening skills while exposing them to information about other nations of the world.

While this project was originally developed for an advanced placement macroeconomics class, it equally applies to a speech class. Each student is asked to select one country in the world other than the United States and prepare a ten-minute presentation on the country. The presenta-

tion is to include the following information:

Political: type of government, head of state, alliances, voting, etc.

Economic: gross national product, per capita income, economic production, major exports/imports, currency, exchange rate, etc.

Cultural/Social: literacy rate, educational system, society composition including ethnic minorities, infant mortality, life expectancy, etc.

Students are encouraged to bring something typical of their country—either a costume, flag, souvenirs or food. Some students brought multiple items, but the vast majority included food samples. This sparked class interest and even cut the absentee rate. Everyone entered class asking: "What do we have to eat today?"

Students are permitted to read their presentation but are encouraged to use note cards. Grading factors can include: research, organization, presentation, use of visual or other aids, and use of prescribed time.

Now for the listening skills! Prior to the presentations a matrix is prepared by the teacher. Rows are for countries while columns will be used for country data. The teacher can begin the process by listing information for the United States in the first row. (See data.) Remaining rows are blank. Students are to listen to the country presentations and write in the country presented on each row and fill in columns with that country's data. At the end of the oral presentations, they will be able to compare the United States with the other countries presented. The teacher could spot-check these matrixes at the end of each period to ensure that listeners are filling in the blanks and not copying them from someone else after class.

The best sources of information are: *Kaleidoscope* (formerly called *Deadline Data on World Affairs*), the United States State Department *Background Notes*, and *The World Almanac*. Other sources could include: *the Statesman Yearbook, Statistical Abstract of the United States* (latest year), an appropriate encyclopedia and subject files of the library.

The following data were gathered concerning the United States: 1988 GNP: $4.864 trillion; 1987 per capita GNP: $18,295; 1989 estimated U.S. population: 247,498,000; Population/square mile: 68; 1988 budget: $1.032 trillion; Percent of government expenditures: defense-25.76%, education-1.74%, health-11.5%, social security and welfare-28.42%; Type of government: representative democracy; Head of state: George Bush; U.S. area: 3,618,770 square miles; Distribution: 20.72% crop land, 26.4% permanent pasture, 28.93% forest and woodlands, 24.01% other; Arable land: 21%; Major cities: New York, Los Angeles, Chicago, Houston, Philadelphia; Life expectancy: males 71.3, females 78.8; Population growth rate: 0.9%; Infant mortality: 10/1000; Illiteracy rate: 1%; Major products: Minerals—coal, copper, lead, molybdenum, phosphates, bauxite, gold, iron, silver, tungsten, zinc; Livestock—cattle, pigs, and sheep; Major agricultural products—corn, wheat, cotton, tobacco, fruits; 1987 imports: $424 billion; Exports: $250.4 billion; Major trading partners: Canada, Japan, and Mexico; Member of the following major organizations: United Nations, NATO, OAS, GATT, and IMF.

This activity provides students with significant topics on which to speak, a guide to research, and a comprehensive listening opportunity. Students are able to grow in these skills while also learning more about the world in which they live.

James Corey

Creativity Vs. "My Speech Is About Avocados"

Goal: To encourage students to think, design, and execute an interesting, creative speech on any topic.

Beginning speech students have a tendency to start their speech with the phrase, "My speech is about..." The substance of the speech will frequently be reminiscent of an encyclopedia article, and the typical ending may contain a variation of: "And that's all the information I could find on . . ." Last year, I found the following assignment successful in helping students to discover original ways to look at a topic.

I passed around an envelope filled with broad topics such as snow, oatmeal, tomatos, pizza, lamp shades, conforming, spam, jail, trust, brand names, football, e.s.p., siblings, space, stereotypes, etc. Each student was instructed to pick three topics and put two back. Students were given the following instructions: "Please prepare a 2 to 3 minute speech on this topic. Try to be creative in your approach and attempt to interest your audience."

The students immediately began protesting that they couldn't possibly plan a speech around their given topic. Before this negative attitude could solidify, I utilized the modeling process to teach them how to examine their topic. I wrote "pencils" on the board and divided the students into small groups. Each was told to brainstorm all aspects of this topic and create a speech. Then one student from each group was chosen to deliver the speech to the class.

Many of the speeches detailed the various purposes of the pencil. One unusual speech was in the form of a rhyming poem.

Another speech began:

"Look at the person on either side of you. Did you know that it's possible for them to get lead poisoning in the next five years? This can happen from the multipurpose utensil called the pencil."

Another began:

"I'm losing my head. I feel so rejected and lonely. No one wants me anymore. Someone chewed off my end and I'm nothing but a stubby piece of wood."

We used these speeches to discuss what makes a speech appealing or dull. Did they have beginnings and endings? Was it just the thoughts that were important, or did the language make a difference? Was it better to discuss one aspect in depth, or lightly treat the whole gamut of possibilities? Now the students had a week to consider all possibilities for their speeches while we worked on another project in class.

Generally, the speeches were interesting and many students examined the subject matter in an unusual or unexpected fashion. One student gave an entertaining speech on siblings with a life-size doll propped up in front of her. Another student gave an incisive speech on the dangers children encounter on Halloween when sick people stuff razor blades into apples. However, I still remember that a very dull speech on avocados (types, where grown, other name, sizes and shapes) elicited my surprise. "Why didn't you talk about how we use them?" I asked. Sheepishly, the student confessed he didn't even know what they looked like, much less what we used them for. It was immediately obvious to everyone why this speech seemed dull and specious.

We videotaped this assignment and discussed the speeches while playing back the videotape. When I passed out an evaluation sheet which solicited students' feelings about the speech assignment, the response was overwhelmingly positive.

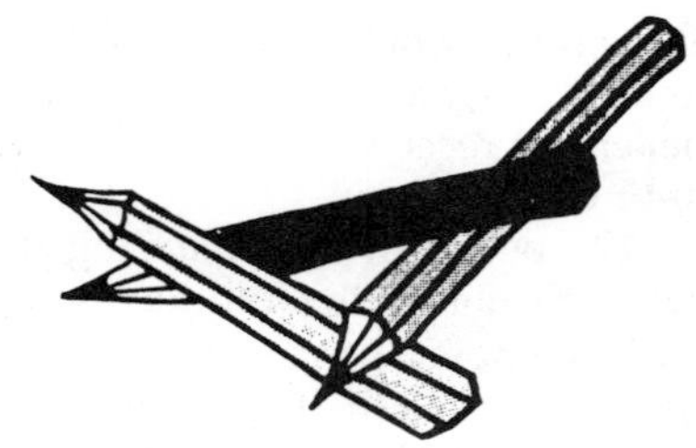

Although the students found it restricting to have to do a speech on a particular subject, most said that this very restriction had forced them to consider all possibilities. While several students originally thought that creative was synonymous with funny, they had also discovered that the issue was not whether the speech was serious or funny, but whether the approach was unique and interesting.

Diane Grainer

Power Minutes

Goal: To offer suggestions for using remaining time at the end of public speaking and argumentation class periods.

We live in a day of power ties, power meetings, power conversations, and power dating. I would like to introduce a new concept for speech teachers - the power minute. One of the difficult challenges facing teachers of public speaking and argumentation courses is what to do with the 5 or 10 minutes remaining at the end of a class period. What alternatives are available when your lecture or classroom presentation is finished before the end of the class period?

In discussing this subject with my students, I noted a number of undesirable alternatives: stretching out a lecture to fit the time limit; excusing the class early; allowing time for students to work on class homework or study for other classes; and wasting the remaining time on idle conversation. These alternatives waste valuable teaching time, lessen instructor control and give the student the impression the teacher is unprepared.

Another alternative to using classroom time involves using power minute presentations. This strategy consists of a brief but significant experience that develops public speaking and critthinking skills. Power minute ical presentations are ungraded, spontaneous activities that allow a few students (or the entire class) to perform a communication task. You may want to consider the following 3 power minute presentations.

Power Panel: This activity begins with selecting 4 or more students to stand (or sit) in the front of the room for an impromptu panel discussion. You should compile a list of discussion questions dealing with local, state, national, or international issues. For example, you want the students to discuss the university parking problem, pollution of beaches, the homeless, or the international trade deficit. You should provide some brief facts and contextual information and a few discussion questions. You should encourage the class to present questions and challenges to the power panel. At the conclusion of the power panel discussion, you should provide a brief summary of questions discussed. This activity encourages critical thinking and an opportunity to assist students in dealing with speech anxiety.

Power Statements: This activity involves participation by every member of the class. You begin the activity by asking each class member to write a paragraph on a specified discussion question or concept. For example, you may want the class to write a paragraph summarizing the most important points to remember in organizing a persuasive speech—or you could present a problem situation for the students to solve. For example, you could request a paragraph on how to solve our nation's increasing college tuition rates. Remember to encourage students to organize their thoughts quickly and to complete the paragraph by the end of the class period. Students' power statements can be used as resource material for future power panel presentations. The power statment is one way to provide students with critical writing opportunities.

Power Impromptu: This activity gives students an opportunity to overcome speech anxiety and to think on their feet. The student draws 3 topics and has a moment to gather his/her thoughts before presenting an impromptu speech based on one of the topics selected. For example, a student may be given these quotations dealing with time:

Time was - Time shall be - drain the glass - But where in Time is now? (John Quincy Adams, "The Hour Glass")

Time goes, you say? Ah no! Alas, Time stays, we go. (Austin Dobson, "The Paradox of Time")

Backward, turn backward, O Time, in your flight, Make me a child again just for tonight! (Elizabeth A. Allen, "Rock Me to Sleep")

The student will review these quotations and select one to use as a basis for the speech. The power impromptu gives students an opportunity to focus more on ideas than delivery. It also provides students with an ungraded, relaxed speaking situation.

The power minute presentation is one solution to every speech teacher's concern about what to do with the last few minutes of class. I found that my students began to look forward to the end-of-class power minute presentations. Some students would come to class with suggested topics and ideas. Power minute presentations encourage critical thinking, creative thought, and enhance public speaking and writing skills. Benjamin Franklin said, "Do not squander time, for that is the stuff life is made of." He would have liked this activity.

Reed Markham

Nomination Speech: The Ideal Date

Goal: To introduce a specific type of speech, to have the students practice this, and finally to make learning enjoyable through the relaxed and humorous nature of the presentations.

My Introduction to Speech class always has twenty students in it, and that number permits only six or seven major, graded speeches. Since other significant types of speeches are not covered, I have made up an assignment on one that can be introduced and practiced the same class period.

I feel that students need to know how to give a nomination speech, even though there is no time for treating it as one of the major assignments. To give a credible introduction to this speech type, I do the following:

I give a mini-lecture on the speech, basing my remarks on Monroe's motivated sequence. I give each student a handout explaining the assignment and the way the motivated sequence relates to nomination speeches. The handout serves as information source, directions, and worksheet.

I next elaborate on the directions printed at the top of the handout: "Nominate someone as an ideal date to be asked out on reverse week-end or on double reverse week-end. Follow the motivated sequence." Since reverse week-end, where the females ask out the males is a campus reality, that part of the assignment makes it realistic for my students.

Divide the class into pairs, with a male and a female in each pair as far as possible. I do my pairings at random so the students will see I have no set couples in mind. I also establish a relaxed, informal atmosphere where no one feels threatened.

When the pairs are together, I review the five motivated sequence steps again, stressing their nomination speech applications. Then I give examples of how the nomination speech can be specifically a date nomination speech. (The students give the expected moans and groans but are by now obviously beginning to enjoy the assignment.)

I give each pair about ten minutes to interview each other to find information to fill in the worksheets for the two-minute date nomination speeches that are to follow. Each student concentrates on getting the appropriate information from his/her partner to complete each section of the motivated sequence.

Even though the speeches are not graded, I sense that each student wants to make a good speech, trying to combine real information with humor in keeping with the relaxed tone of the assignment.

Both students in a pair go up front. The one being nominated sits in a chair; the one doing the nominating stands up close by. Making reference to the notes just taken on the person being nominated, the students talk for two minutes to persuade the male or female students in class to ask out the person being nominated. As soon as the first nominator has finished, the two students change places: the speaker sits down and the nominee stands up to give a speech about the other.

Although I do not give grades for this speech, a teacher certainly could. I feel the intrinsic learning of the whole process is justification enough. Students seem to enjoy themselves as much on this day as on any during the term, yet they have been introduced to the process of nominating a person for an office, have practiced this process, and have entertained each other as a bonus.

In summary, I find the nomination speech process as described above to be educational and entertaining. What more could we as teachers ask?

Wilma McClarty

The "Jeopardy" of Impromptu Speaking

Goal: To give students a chance to develop impromptu speaking skills in a relatively non-stressful situation.

The skill of being able to make a clear, concise impromptu speech is one which would benefit any student. In our ever-expanding communicative environment, one doesn't always have the time to prepare a speech carefully. Rather, one often must speak on short notice without the leisure of lengthy preparation.

To give my students the chance to improve their impromptu skills, I structure several class days around the television show "Jeopardy." I place this activity at the end of the semester so that students have a good understanding of both informative and persuasive speaking. This also helps to end the class on a positive, light-hearted note. (Some teachers may find this is an activity they can conduct periodically throughout an advanced public speaking course with the final round occurring on the last day of class.)

Here are the things I do to prepare for this event.

1. Before class, I develop impromptu categories along the same lines of "Jeopardy," including "Current World Events," "Sports," "Campus Controversy," "Music," and "Good but Inexpensive Restaurants." I use a standard piece of posterboard on which I print the categories as column headings across the top. The long side of the board is in the horizontal position.

2. Under each category I place five 3 x 5" notecards. On these cards I write theses for speeches in all categories. For example, under "Current Events" a thesis for a speech might be "The United States should/should not protect foreign tankers in the Persian Gulf," or "Television evangelism: fraud or legitimate?"

3. I tape the notecards under each topic with the message side hidden from view. Each card contains a number from 10 to 50. I place the lowest numbered card (10) closest to the top (as in the actual TV show). The highest numbered card (50) goes at the bottom. Students learn that the cards with the highest point value will have the most difficult thesis statement.

Before the competition begins, I make sure each student has a good understanding of how to make an impromptu speech. I have my students use a method derived from Eugene White's *Practical Public Speaking* (New York: MacMillan Publishing Co., 1982). This format includes four steps: 1. *Point Step*—the speaker tells the audience what s/he hopes to accomplish in the speech; 2. *Reason Step*—the speaker states a reason why the point s/he is using is a valid one; 3. *Evidence Step*—the speaker gives suporting ideas for the reason step, and 4. *Restatement of Point Step.*

When students are called on, they select a category at any level of difficulty. I act as game show host by reading out the category, the point total the student selects, and the thesis statement. After reading the thesis statement aloud to the class, I hand the notecard to the student. The student uses this card during the next 3 to 4 minutes while preparing to speak. In the meantime, I replace that card with another one of equal value to insure that all students have equal choices in topics and levels of difficulty.

The student goes to the front of the class and presents a speech on the chosen topic without using any notes. Each student receives two scores from me: 1. a score from 10 to 50 on the effectiveness and clarity of the speech, and 2. a score based on the difficulty of the category chosen which always will be a constant score. For example, if a student selected a topic with a difficulty level of 40 points, automatically s/he receives 40 points which will be added to my evaluation score.

At the end of the session, the student with the highest score receives a "Master of Impromptu Speaking Degree" which I produce from a certificate-making program on my personal computer. If a tie results, the remaining speakers compete in a "talk off."

Bruce C. McKinney

Painless Impromptu Speaking

Goal: To facilitate intrinsically motivated impromptu speaking and illustrate the importance of effective listening in problem solving.

One of the first challenges faced in teaching the basic speech course seems to be stimulating spontaneous student communication in a nonthreatening environment. A technique that can be helpful in achieving this goal is cooperative impromptu problem solving (CIPS).

Shortly after the class begins, discuss forms of speech preparation and delivery. Next, complete the CIPS activity outlined below.

1. The instructor briefly describes a fictitious situation which has elements of mystery. Two typical situations might be:
   a. It is a dark and stormy night. A large mansion is situated on a bluff overlooking the sea. The wind is blowing, lightning is flashing and thunder is crashing. The butler is walking down a dimly lighted hall of the house when he hears a sound coming from the area of the bathroom. He goes to investigate, and is shocked to find Tom and Mary dead on the floor of the bathroom. Broken glass is on the floor. The window is open and the curtains are blowing inward.
   b. Bill is running home. Before he reaches home he is confronted by a man who is wearing a mask. The man has a blunt object in his hand. When Tom sees this man, he turns around and runs as fast as he can in the opposite direction.
2. Students, as a class, are to determine specifically what has happened in the situation described, by asking the instructor questions which can be answered only with a "yes" or "no" response.
3. The instructor emphasizes that: the questions are to be spontaneous, any question is a good question, and although participation is voluntary, it is encouraged for all.
4. Students are urged to listen carefully to their classmates' questions, and to the instructor's responses.
5. The activity culminates when the impromptu questions and effective listening result in the discovery of what the situation actually involved. At this point, the instructor can discuss with the class how listening may have impacted on the problem solving process. (The solution for the first situation is that Tom and Mary are *fish*. The wind blowing in through the open window knocked their fish bowl off the counter and it fell on the floor, breaking into pieces. The glass and liquid on the floor are from the bowl, and Tom and Mary, poor souls, died of suffocation. The solution for the second situation is that Bill is playing baseball, and is trying to run from third base to home plate. Before he can get "home," he is confronted by the catcher wearing his catcher's mask and carrying the baseball, which is the blunt object.)

Students appear to enjoy this activity. They are challenged to discover the answer to the mystery, and enjoy the "trick" nature of the situations.

The CIPS technique is a good motivator and "icebreaker." I have had occasions when the class broke into spontaneous applause upon solving a mystery situation. The technique can motivate even the most reticent students to communicate their ideas voluntarily in an impromptu setting. The class also has an opportunity to work together in solving a problem by using speaking and listening skills. Student awareness of the practical importance of listening in the oral communication process increases as a result of this exercise.

Ed Purdy

Structure And Substance In A One-Minute Speech

Goal: To provide students with an understanding of the substantive elements of rhetoric and increase structured speaking opportunities by using one-minute speeches.

Approach, State, Develop, Leave: these words, along with the communication concepts of Attention-Getters, Ethos, and Self-Interest, became the litany of my speech communication students this past semester. I have adapted John P. Ryan's idea of the one-minute speech (*The Communication Quarterly*, 34, 433) to provide students with a structured way to: 1. increase the number of speeches they are able to deliver and evaluate, 2. reduce speaker apprehension, and

3. make the substantive elements and organizational structure of speaking "second nature" to my students.

Students are given the basic structure of a speech (introduction, body, and conclusion) with an explanation of the function of each part and the primary elements which should be included. The *Approach* is to include an attention-getter, one's ethos, and an explanation of how the audience will benefit from the speech. A *Statement of the Controlling Idea(s)* completes the introduction of the speech. Students *Develop* the idea, or the body of the speech. Finally, they *Leave* the idea by making a summary statement which is the conclusion of the speech.

Since these generally take the form of impromptu speeches, students have less anxiety because the time between receiving the assignment and delivering the speech is reduced. Yet, students are planning and presenting speeches, as opposed to merely stringing sentences together and talking.

I adapt the one-minute speech by asking students to write topics that I collect and randomly distribute, requesting that speeches be prepared in three minutes. Also, I use the idea for two-minute speeches to demonstrate some of the ideas of information exchange. Students select an object for a topic, exchange topics, and create speeches in which they are not allowed to disclose what their object is. Rather, they have to explain it. The class tries to guess the object described.

A third way I use Ryan's concept is as a class exercise in preparation for the student speeches to persuade. I divide the class into groups of four to five students and have them work together in preparing a persuasive speech. One member of each group delivers the speech and it is evaluated. This helps build students' confidence in their understanding and ability to apply the elements they are to use in their graded presentations. It also helps to identify problems my students have and enables me to clarify them before they give their graded speeches. This results in presentations of a higher quality.

I recommend one-minute speeches as building blocks in the reinforcement of concepts discussed in class. They allow the teacher to comment more fully on the speeches and on communication factors discussed in class and demonstrated in the speeches. Also, they can increase the number of public presentations and the quality of speeches. Finally, they can reduce communication apprehension and help to make careful speech organization a habit, rather than just a class assignment.

Allison Schumer

Me? Give An Impromptu Speech? No Way!

Goal: To decrease students' apprehension about giving an impromptu speech while increasing their understanding of the evaluation process.

Although students give several ungraded impromptu speeches in my public speaking classes, when the time comes to *grade* this speech, I find the anxiety level rises. I begin grading impromptu speeches about half-way through the semester. I do these speeches at the end of class when I find I have extra time, so these speeches go on for a couple of weeks. This semester, I tried a new approach which worked extremely well. I found that the anxiety level dropped significantly and students enjoyed the assignment while learning the skills and responsibilities of evaluating another person's speech. Although students had critiqued every speech since the beginning of the semester, they discovered being responsible for a person's grade added a new element.

I divided the class into groups of 5-7 people by having them count off (to avoid allowing the same people to work together each time). Their task was to develop, in 1½ hours, the impromptu speaking assignment—all elements: topics, time limit, and evaluation criteria. The only guidelines were that the speech must be graded, using the same point system I use in class; each student, as well as the teacher, must be responsible for a percentage of the final grade, and the final product will be a combination of each group's efforts. Then I combined the information they gave me and produced the following assignment sheet.

IMPROMPTU SPEECH

1. *Topic* - You will draw 3 topics from those the class has chosen. These are topics you will be able to discuss without going beyond your own knowledge and experience. Then you will select 1 topic out of the 3 for the subject of your speech. You will be allowed 3 minutes to prepare. (Notes are optional)
2. *Time* - There is no time limit.
3. *Grading* - 35 points possible. Criteria for grading: execution, 7 points; creativity, 6 points; facial expressions, 6 points; eye contact, 4 points; enthusiasm, 3 points; poise/composure, 3 points; voice, 3 points; gestures, 3 points.

Each audience member will be grading your impromptu speech, using the above criteria. Half of your final grade will be an average of the class grading and half, will be from the instructor for a total of 35 points.

You will be called to give your speeches in the order in which you signed up. If you are not present, you will be put at the end of the list to be called again. No penalty will be given. If you are called to give your speech and you refuse to go, no credit will be given unless extenuating circumstances exist which will be determined by the instructor.

4. *Evaluations* - You will turn in an evaluation for every impromptu speaker except yourself. The criteria listed above

will be used. On your paper, put your name, the speaker's name, and then list the criteria. After the speech you will award the points earned in each category and make any desired comments.

5. *Beginning Date* - Impromptu speeches will begin April 6.

On index cards, I wrote each topic the class had selected. I collected the evaluation sheets from the students at the end of each class. After removing the evaluator's name, I attached the classes' evaluations to my evaluation so the student was able to see all the points earned and the final grade.

The class was very receptive and enthusiastic about this project. Students' comments inlcuded such things as: it was their favorite topic in class; how much easier the impromptu speech was than they expected; how being responsible for someone else's grade was not quite what they anticipated; and how important it was to know and understand the criteria. After the last impromptu speech was completed, we discussed and evaluated the results of the project as a class.

Jeanette Wall

Two Birds with One Stone

Goal: To give students practice communicating effectively while using a visual aid.

Recently, in a beginning speech class, I "taught" the use of visual aids by conducting a surprise workshop. I gave students five minutes to select something they had with them about which they could develop a one to two minute speech using the object as a visual aid. For those who were completely stumped, I provided some items from my office: a box of tissue, a yellow legal pad, a bottle of white-out, etc.

One student, using her Vuarnet sunglasses, talked about the dangers of looking into the sun and the value of investing in quality dark glasses. Another, effectively demonstrating the ease and accessibility of his backpack, talked about things to look for when shopping for a pack of one's own.

Even the less successful speeches provided animated discussion during the critique period. Students were able to identify the differences between a "good" and "bad" visual: the bottle of white-out was too small; the photograph, passed around the room, was distracting, etc.

One of the students gave a creative speech about how brand names are substituted for generic terms. He began by holding a box of tissue and asking, "What is this?" The answer, of course, was "kleenex." A problem developed when, as he spoke, the student continually pulled tissues from the box. Initially effective, the repetition of this action, and the resulting pile of tissue, became humorous and detracted from the speech. That led to a discussion of how to cope with an unanticipated situation.

This experiment, which far exceeded my expectations, allowed me to combine practice using a visual aid and with impromptu speech making.

Dorothy Wilks

Speech Assignments—Introductory/ "Ice-Breaker" Speeches

VITAL SPEECHES

VOL. LIV, No. 22 — SEPTEMBER 1, 1988 — TWICE A MONTH

The Truth About Savings and Loan Institutions — Theo H. Pitt, Jr.
Restructuring America — T. Boone Pickens, Jr.
Japan and West Germany — Arthur Burck
Hostile Takeovers in America Today — A. William Reynolds
Sick Companies Don't Have to Die — C. Charles Bahr
Myths and Truths, but No Challenge — Robert B. Horton
A Loaf of Bread — Bet T. Craig
Ethical Leaders — Ronald W. Roskens
Africa — America — Ja A. Jahannes
A Bank By Any Other Name — Thomas G. Labrecque
The Enemies of Responsible Communication — W. Charles Redding

IMPARTIAL • CONSTRUCTIVE • AUTHENTIC

Using Vital Speeches of the Day In the Introductory Speech Classroom

Goal: To provide students with practice in oral interpretation of oratory and an understanding of various rhetorical styles and strategies.

Recently, I began using *Vital Speeches* in my Introduction to Speech Communication class. In the past, I had used it only as a resource from which to draw sample speeches for students to respond to in a written critique. Although this still remains a useful exercise, my new use of the transcripted speeches allows my students to gain extra performance practice.

My class is structured so the first 2 student presentations remain ungraded in order to keep beginning speaker anxiety at a minimum. After the traditional speech of self-introduction, generally I have given some type of oral performance of prose assignment. Past exercises included having students simulate evening newscasts with excerpts from the newspaper. I also tried the "free choice" approach, encouraging students to bring in a favorite selection from a novel or short story to share in a more formally delivered fashion. I even tried having students act out excerpts from Socrates' plea to the Athenian jury from the *Trial and Death of Socrates.* Each had its drawbacks: newscasters used the same cliche transitions; students said they either didn't have a favorite piece of prose or didn't own any appropriate books; and many students complained the "old fashioned" language of Plato limited their ability to understand his material.

As an alternative assignment, I asked students to go to the library and look through several issues of *Vital Speeches* to find a transcript of a talk that excited them and encouraged them to reflect on the speaker's thesis. They were to photocopy the speech and rehearse delivering a 5 minute passage. Also, they were required to introduce the passage as part of their presentation, describe what is known about the occasion, time, and setting of the original talk, and explain what central message the speaker was striving to communicate. The students then attempted to deliver the excerpt in a manner they believed would "do justice" to the intent of the original orators.

Topics that students selected to share included citizenship and responsibility, the drug problem, leadership in management, star wars defense, air traffic control, agriculture, liberal education, technological advancement, the changing role of women, and developing creativity. One student elected to share a speech on immigration policies originally delivered in 1938. He cleverly tied it in to today's immigration issues in his introduction. Although students went to the library at separate times, none of my 40 students selected the same speech. We had a nice diversity of subjects around which to build a discussion.

This exercise serves several functions and has several advantages. First, the students seemed genuinely excited to be sharing a message that inspired them personally. Secondly, as an initial assignment, students have a chance to experiment with different delivery styles without the added risk of self-disclosing their own words and composition. The content of the selections sparked some nice in-class discussion as the presenting student continued to champion the cause of the selected orator.

In sum, this is a useful classroom assignment and one that students seem to enjoy.

Helen Meldrum

Brush with Greatness

Goal: To create a non-threatening, positive class atmosphere and introduce class members to each other.

This activity was inspired by the television show "Late Night with David Letterman." Letterman occasionally runs a segment titled "Brush with Greatness." Audience members describe incidents about famous people with whom they have had contact.

In class, students are encouraged to tell stories about meeting celebrities, attending well known events, or visiting famous places. This activity adds a personal touch to class. Students have described contacts ranging from fishing with John Wayne to meeting the Emperor of Japan.

This exercise has many advantages for the students and the class as a whole. First, the activity allows the students to introduce themselves in a casual, personal way. This lets the audience associate the speaker with something with which everyone can relate. People seem to have a certain fascination with famous entities.

Second, this exercise allows the students to ''loosen up'' in the classroom. It is an icebreaking activity for the students that provides topics for

Washington, D.C.

informal conversations that may take place in the future.

''Brush with Greatness'' is a favorite activity of my students. The stories that my students tell are as interesting as they are unpredictable. To maintain the non-threatening nature of the activity, no grades are given. This assignment allows students to get to know each other and to be more relaxed when it comes time to do more structured speeches.

Sean Raftis

The Personal Experience Speech In Public Speaking

Goal: To use a simple structure, a clear-cut thesis statement, as well as conversational delivery in the first prepared speech.

I believe students benefit from gradually working into full-scale public speaking, as well as coping with the pressure of having the speech graded. Consequently, each of my students participates in two impromptu speeches of two minutes length. Then they prepare a speech which I comment on in written form before they do a graded speech.

We begin with the personal experience speech. It is five minutes long and has two parts. One part, which usually is the first and longest part, requires students to describe one personal experience, or a series of related events, which taught them a significant lesson. The second part is a statement and amplification of the lesson. A proverb or quotation may be used to amplify the lesson statement.

I suggest that students approach their search for a topic in three ways.

1. List an important lesson you have learned. Think back to an experience or a series of related experiences which taught that lesson. (One also could learn the lesson vicariously from someone else's recounting of an event.)

2. Alternately, one can try to list experiences which have made a vivid impression. Analyze which of these taught a worthwhile lesson.

3. If the first two approaches yield nothing, study some proverbs or quotations. Any that you have a strong feeling about probably relate to learning an important lesson. Try to recall the related experience(s).

While students are working on this speech, we do a two-minute impromptu speech in which each student selects a proverb to attack or defend.

As a beginning speech, the personal experience format has several values. First, it teaches a simple two-topic structure. Second, students can see that a sentence summarizing the lesson learned is the thesis of the speech. Third, getting used to using one or more proverbs or quotations to amplify the lesson, perhaps as an impressive introduction or conclusion, is a good technique to learn early. Fourth, the student should require few, if any, notes to present this speech; hence, getting started with the ideal of a direct and conversational delivery.

This series yields some unusual and thoughtful topics. For instance, one of my students told how he had watched the quiz show, "Fandango," on the Nashville Network. He decided he could do as well as the contestants. He vowed to get on the show. Later, he did, and he won $10,000 in prizes. His lesson was, "Confidence and determination eventually will pay off." Another student related her early problems with dyslexia. At first, school officials recommended putting her in an institution for the retarded. Her mother wouldn't hear of this, and insisted that she be tested until the exact problem was isolated. The girl's lesson was, "No one will persist in taking up for you like your mother."

Valerie L. Schneider

Interviewing: A Triadic Exercise

Goal: To strengthen the student's interviewing skills and provide an "ice breaker"speech.

As an instructor for a survey-type basic speech course, I have come to appreciate exercises that tie together multiple communication topics. These exercises often underscore the relationships between seemingly divergent areas of communication study. The triadic interview is one such exercise. It works as an interpersonal ice-breaker for students, a first speaking experience, and as the introduction or conclusion to a discussion of interviewing principles or listening behaviors.

The instructor may choose to preface this exercise with a brief discussion of interviewing principles, including types of questions (open or closed, primary or secondary) and their significance, interview schedules, note-taking, and so on. This discussion can provide an excellent lead-in to the following exercise.

First, students write out 10 open-ended, primary questions that they believe someone else might ask in order to "really" get to know them. As you might expect, this often takes students several minutes and the overall depth of questions varies from student to student. Having allowed 10-15 minutes, I then distribute another sheet of paper asking each student to record 5 or more questions that s/he believes an interviewer might ask in order to know him/her better.

Next, students break into groups of 3, preferably with fellow students they do not know well. Once they are in these triads, students exchange questions. The process is simple: Person A takes the questions written by Person B; Person B takes the questions written by Person C; and Person C takes the questions written by Person A. The immediate objective is for students to use this question schedule in an interview of the person who wrote it. The overall objective is to prepare, and deliver to the class, an introduction of the person interviewed. This introduction is 2-4 minutes long and requires each student to do a bit of "digging" in the interview.

These interviews are conducted in class. On the one occasion when students are neither interviewer or interviewee, they act as observers. In the observer role, students listen carefully to what is transpiring between the other members of the triad, recording their own observations of interview performance.

When the 3 interviews are completed, students are asked to evaluate and comment briefly on the interview they observed.

The final 2 steps in this exercise are preparation and delivery of the actual introductions. Generally, I review the key components of a good introduction and allow students out-of-class preparation time.

This exercise has been interesting and rewarding for my students (expanding on the more traditional dyadic exercise). At the same time, it is a very fine introduction to interviewing. This is particularly significant to me, as an instructor, because often I require students to do at least one outside interview in order to get supporting material for a later speech. In this way, I can stress the value of interviewing skills and multiple speech support sources.

In addition, each student, in the capacity of observer, acts as a listener and critic. Listening and feedback skills are an integral part of the basic course.

Used early in the semester, this exercise underscores the value of good listening as a prerequisite to effective and useful feedback. The exercise also allows students to provide "performance" feedback in a small group setting, nicely prefacing the general class feedback sessions that follow each round of public speaking. Finally, the speaking phase of the exercise allows students another (perhaps a first) opportunity to speak.

This exercise, then, emphasizes a variety of communication skills in multiple settings. It can be a very beneficial experience for students in the basic course.

Scott Smithson

The Analogy Speech

Goal: To provide an initial speaking assignment in Public Speaking which is memorable for the class and provides the speaker with practice in effective organization and delivery.

The first speaking assignment may be the most difficult assignment in the public speaking course. Students face the challenging task of presenting their first public address to classmates as well as an instructor, who evaluates their performance. The instructor faces an equally challenging task: designing an assignment that achieves two purposes.

1. The first speech often is used to introduce each student, ideally in a memorable way. When students get to know each other, they often find the speech act less threatening. Indeed, introductory speeches can facilitate a congenial and supportive classroom atmosphere. They also provide information for the audience analyses recommended for future speeches.

2. The first speaking assignment should enable students to practice the rudiments of effective delivery and organization. It should get students "on their feet and talking" *in an effective manner,* rather than provide the opportunity for practice of ineffective behavior. Further, a good first round of speeches can provide positive models of effective speech making.

The analogy speech can be used as a first assignment to achieve these purposes. It is a two-to-four minute speech-of-introduction in which the speaker introduces him/herself to the audience through the use of an analogy. The student compares him/herself to any real or fictional thing except another person (see sample outlines below).

Sally's House Cat

My name is Sally and I'm like your average American house cat.

MP1: require a lot of time alone to pursue my own interests

MP2: very affectionate and loving to my friends and family when I choose to spend time with them

My name is Sally and I'm like your average American house cat.

John's Sailboat

My name is John and I'm like a sailboat.

MP1: tossed and turned in the wind; must fight for control

MP2: when the sailor learns to control the ship, it becomes a precision instrument, working in harmony with nature

My name is John and I'm like a sailboat.

The logistics of the assignment are simple. The instructor assigns the speech during the first week of class. Discussion and preparation for the assignment require no more than thirty minutes of class time. Each student volunteers to introduce him/herself to the class at some time during the next two weeks. Four or five speeches are delivered per class period. During the balance of the period, the instructor discusses material typically presented during the first weeks of the course.

Students receive written critiques on four aspects of speech making: *eye contact* (Did the speaker look at the audience more than 50% of the time?); *voice* (Did the speaker speak loudly enough to be heard clearly in the back of the room?); *timing* (Did the speech fit within the minimum and maximum time limits?); *organizational pattern* (Did the speaker employ the required organizational pattern: an introduction containing the speaker's name and his/her thesis statement positing the analogy, two main points of support that explain the analogy, and a conclusion that restates the speaker's name and thesis?).

Lynne Webb

Testing and Evaluation

Grading Student Speeches: An Experiential Approach

Goal: To increase usefulness of student speeches as instructional models while evaluating with pertinent, contemporary standards.

Scan the pages of any recent speech journal and it is obvious that speech criticism has moved far beyond the traditional models and precepts of neo-Aristotelianism. However, speech classroom texts and practice remain firmly rooted in that work. Granted, the vast literature stretching from the pre-Socratics to Wichelns has much to offer, but the mass-mediated contemporary environment makes it obvious that no rhetorical theory should be held absolute. In discussing eclectic experiential criticism, Professor Robert L. Scott points out that "an infinite number of concepts, strategies, and postures are available for the study of the rhetorical act," and "close interaction between the critic and the act itself is necessary" if we are to select the most appropriate theoretical framework for any given situation.

The most common and far-reaching effect of neo-Aristotelian speech theory in the classroom today is likely to be found in the evaluation forms most of us use to grade student speeches. We compose our own forms and alter them from time to time to reflect changes in our personal conceptual frameworks. Such forms simplify evaluation and minimize time spent assigning grades. Because the typical speech class is likely to have precious little time to complete all assigned speeches, such time-saving devices are always attractive.

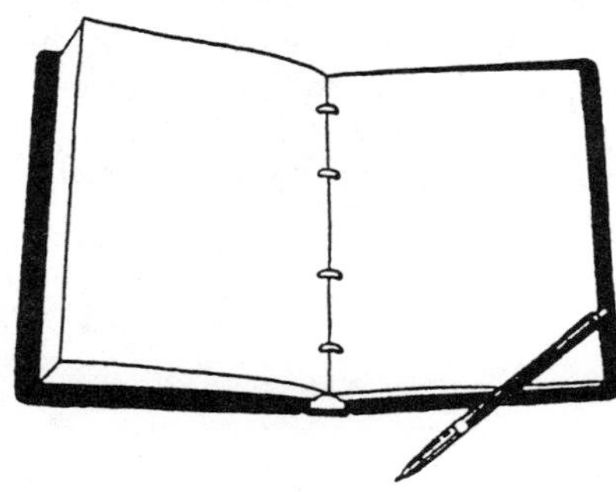

It is inevitable, however, that the categories on our evaluation sheets imply a fixed standard, an ideal speech form toward which students tacitly aspire. Especially at the secondary level, firm standards for organization, argument, style, and so on are pedagogically useful, but consider that flexible standards surely must be more so. The sheer existence of electronic mediation demands that our students explore an enormous variety of message options with as little bias toward any particular critical framework as possible. What is most important, especially at the beginning levels, is that skill at and sensitivity to *effectiveness* in communication be developed.

Consider Scott's comparison of traditional and experiential critical approaches in *Methods in Rhetorical Criticism:* "To the traditional rhetorical critic, to judge justly was the preferred end of critical action (even though description was quite often the way-station achieved). To the experiential critic, to interpret openly in such a way as to encourage further individual interpretations seems preferable." The traditional rating form is all too often a quantified description: a map or graph contrasting the student's speech to an implied ideal. As an experiential alternative, why not use a blank piece of paper upon which the teacher records the stream-of-thought experience he or she has during each speech?

By recording their own reactions, teachers identify precisely those aspects of a speech from which the class can best further its learning. With good planning and a little practice, discussion following each speech will replace abstract reading and lectures, examining concrete events the audience has actually just experienced. The teacher's stream-of-thought record reflects a mixture of content and process automatically proportioned to emphasize whatever the speech experience teaches best.

But what about feedback? We all hold that students should be told their strengths and shortcomings, both to facilitate improvement and to justify grades. Post-speech discussion in class provides the most powerful feedback by focusing on the experience the audience has just had, and the teacher who has just shared the experience is best equipped to lead the discussion. Every attempt should be made to emphasize the positive aspects of each presentation, leaving negatives to be noted in writing during the assignment of a grade.

The experiential grading procedure involves two steps. After all the speeches of a round are given and all required documentation (bibliographies, outlines, etc.) collected, step one asks teachers to review each speech and to list strengths and weaknesses or "well-dones" and "work-ons" on the evaluation page just below the stream-of-consciousness notes. This list reflects evaluation primarily derived from the experience as recalled rather than from comparison to any preconceived system. Given well-developed in-class discussion about a speech, strength and weakness comments listed on the evaluation page will carry the weight of audience opinion as well as document a high level of teacher concern. Most important, the stream-of-consciousness record is evidence that the teacher has really listened and is basing the grade on experience the student speech actually produced.

Step two involves nothing more than sorting the evaluation sheets with attached documentation into piles and rating the piles according to whatever scoring system the teacher prefers. For example, my basic classes require four speeches, each counting more than the last: the first is 15 points, second 20, third 25, and the last counts 30 points. Typically, first speeches fall into five piles rated 11, 12, 13, 14, and, for the top one or two presentations, 15. For the last speech, the range may dip as low as 21 or 22, permitting considerably more discrimination.

With practice, the experiential method takes no more time than the traditional rating of categories. By focusing on *having* the experience rather than on rating it, the teacher both promotes a realistic contemporary view of effective communication and harnesses directly student experience as a path to learning.

W. Lance Haynes

Sanctioned "Cheating" on Exams

Goal: To enhance student mastery of course concepts for exams.

For several years, I have legalized "cheating" on exams in every course that I teach. Included in the syllabus is the following statement: "Important note: for each exam, you will be allowed to use both sides of a 4"x6" card or slip of paper as an aid—put anything you want on this 'cheat sheet'."

I have found this approach to have several benefits.

1. Students just can't resist the chance to "cheat legally." Virtually all students end up taking advantage of the opportunity; they think they're getting a "good deal," and that the cheat sheet gives them a competitive edge. What they don't realize, of course, is that in the process of preparing this aid, they also are studying it quite carefully—much more carefully than they would probably do otherwise. The cheat sheet motivates them to outline chapters, make judgments about what is important, and consider what they do and do not know. Many students cram so much information onto the card that they tell me they never really use it during the exam—in essence, they've prepared so well that they don't need it.
2. The cheat sheet allows me to ask better questions. Rather than simply asking students to regurgitate lists of terms, I can ask questions which require them to provide examples of a concept, compare and contrast ideas, or critically analyze an idea. One need not ask these more "sophisticated" questions in an essay format—all the exams I use are some combination of true-false, multiple choice, and very short answer questions.
3. From a purely pragmatic standpoint, I get far fewer complaints from students about questions that are too "picky" or unfair. I tell them that if they have trouble remembering the Latin term for that fallacy in reasoning, or the technical name for that problem in communication, they should put it on the card.
4. From a pedagogical and philosophical standpoint, I think the legal cheat sheet is in keeping with current trends in our culture. We live in an age where "information retrieval" and the ability to manipulate ideas have become as important as rote memorization. When we were students, we probably resented an instructor who asked us to memorize long lists of terms, so why should we expect others to do it? Of course, I do think that some degree of "internalized knowledge" is essential—that's part of my rationale for limiting students to a 4"x6" card. But I see no compelling reason why students should be required to memorize everything.

If you do experiment with this system, here are a few suggestions. First, remind students about the cheat sheet the day before the exam—most are not accustomed to bringing such an aid with them. (However, they get in the habit very quickly!) Second, stress that the card probably will be most valuable if they put information on it that they have trouble understanding or remembering. Third, I do tell students beforehand that I will still try to challenge and even frustrate them a bit. Since I know that they have notes, I remind them that I will be asking questions that require them to do more than simply "copy" from their card. They deserve to know this.

Finally, for those who, for some reason, are worried that everyone will get a perfect score on exams, I should stress that this system still has real "discriminating power," provided you ask the right kinds of questions. Although I think that students learn more with legally sanctioned cheating, the exam scores in my classes still vary widely. Legalized cheating helps promote a basic understanding of the course material, but my standards for mastery still make As and Bs marks of distinction.

David Lapakko

Essential Pursuit: A Classroom Review Technique

Goal: To help students learn class material and prepare for tests.

To minimize the drudgery of reviewing for an examination, my introductory communication classes play "Essential Pursuit" during the class immediately preceding the exam.

Early in the term, students sign up for one of four teams, and meet in class to choose a coordinator and a name. The coordinator is responsible for convening and moderating out-of-class study sessions. Team names can be as outrageous ("Ungawa") or sophisticated ("Sophists") as the team wishes. Each team meets before the game day to prepare for the contest by reviewing text and lecture material. Team 1 (the Questioners) also prepares 20–25 questions. On "Essential Pursuit" day:

Team 1 (Questioners) ask their questions prepared from the text and lectures. The questions should require short answers and include: multiple-choice, definitions, procedures, true-false, etc. If the answer is "false," the reason must also be supplied. The Questioners stipulate how many points each question is worth, and a different member of the team must ask subsequent questions. One Questioner is Timekeeper; another is Scorekeeper.

Teams 2 and 3 (Contestants) are alternatively asked questions and have one minute to confer before giving a team answer by a different spokesperson for each round. If the answer is incorrect or incomplete, the opposing Contestants are given the same question and have 30 seconds to confer.

Team 4 (Judges) has one minute after the first team answers to decide whether the answer is adequate. The Judges assign appropriate points for partial or full answers. In case of dispute with the Questioners, the Judges have final judgment.

Team roles rotate for subsequent before-exam games, so that each team has the opportunity to play all roles by the end of the term.

An alternative approach is to use a round-robin approach, in which each team prepares questions and roles rotate after every two questions.

I bring to class individual prizes for the team winners: pens, gum, candy bars, homemade cookies, apples from our trees. The real rewards for the students, however, are an entertaining way to review and the glee of winning. I use at least one question from the game in the following exam.

Not only do students enjoy this review method, but they also must use the communication skills learned in class: precise language, reading non-verbal cues, listening (no question or answer can be repeated), conflict resolution, cooperation, leadership, power. Occasionally I interrupt the proceedings to correct misinformation or point out their transactions. It is an effective arena for the students and me to see if they can *apply* interpersonal skills learned in class.

Each class enthusiastically endorses this game. Sample student responses:

—from a senior: "While it's true that the game offers an opportunity for review, it also offers an excellent opportunity for interpersonal communication, and in particular self-disclosure between group members. . . . Only two of us could be considered friends when the group was formed. Now I consider everyone in that group as my friend. Through our organizational meetings and classroom experiences we've really learned a lot about each other."

—from a sophomore: "Today during our Essential Pursuit, I noticed how far everyone in the class has progressed. On day one, no one had any idea of what Interpersonal Communication was. Now, we all apply what we've learned *inside and outside* class. And it makes studying fun."

Nancy Macky

The Oral Quiz, or Letting Students Talk More While You Talk Less

Goal: To give students still more opportunity to speak and to give them a more active role in the learning process by using oral quizzes.

Probably the chief challenge facing every speech teacher is to find time for more speaking opportunities for students. One way I found to save classtime while increasing students' informal oral performances is the oral quiz.

The procedure for this quiz is very simple. At the beginning of the term I tell my students they are responsible for knowing the assigned material in the test, as well as lecture material, but I won't cover the text assignments in class. I assure them that if they have questions about any of the assigned readings, I'll be glad to answer them. Otherwise, they are on their

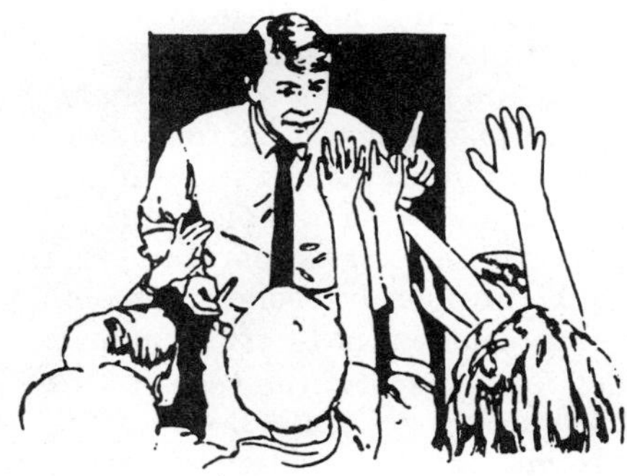

own for covering this material. By doing this, I gain 3 to 4 hours which I can use for speaking assignments. More importantly, the student must play a more active role in the learning process and must be able to verbalize what s/he has learned.

Students answer oral questions, during the 3 to 4 scheduled oral quizzes, which are based on the most important points covered in the text. They remain seated but must project their answers so everyone can hear. After a designated student has provided his/her best answer in a dialogue with me, other students have the opportunity to supplement, clarify or question. Finally, I summarize or elaborate upon the subject to ensure that the students recognize the key points.

I evaluate students' responses by assigning them a plus, check, or minus. At the end of the term, I consider these when I figure the final grade.

The process has worked well for me: students *do* study the text more thoroughly and retain major concepts better than they used to do. They *do* speak more frequently. Furthermore, valuable time is saved for other speech opportunities. We talk a lot today about student-centered classrooms. The oral quiz is another method of operationalizing this idea.

Ellen L. Tripp

Applying Public Speaking Tools in Tests

Goal: To provide students with the opportunity to demonstrate application of the tools of public speaking in test formats.

Although students need to be tested on material read in the text, I also believe their ability to *apply* the same information is important. Oral presentations accomplish this to some extent but I believe some students skip preparation steps—and some simply fail to apply what they are learning. The exams I use require students to show their ability to apply the tools of public speaking.

As reading assignments are made during the semester, I give oral quizzes on each chapter. The students receive a schedule of when quizzes will be given, and on what chapter, at the beginning of the semester. The oral quizzes (5 to 10 objective questions) accomplish several purposes. First, the quizzes increase the students' ability to listen well. I repeat each question as many times as requested to do so. However, once I have moved to the next question, I will not repeat a previous one. During the semester, the number of times I had to repeat questions declined significantly.

I found these quizzes demonstrated only students' ability to recall information, so I developed a midterm and a final exam which required them to apply the information. My students found these exams challenging and much more helpful than just having to memorize material from the text. You can revise the questions easily to fit the length of your class or the material you may want to emphasize. My classes were an hour and a half in length. The midterm exam focused on an informative speech and the final, on a persuasive speech.

The Midterm Exam

This exam is designed to determine whether or not you can apply the tools of Public Speaking to a particular speaking situation, to show you understand the concepts involved. I suggest you read all of the questions before answering any of them.

SITUATION: You have just been introduced at a banquet honoring outstanding students on campus. You are the second of two speakers. The previous speaker was a college administrator who discussed "Excellence in Academic Achievement." He was boring. The awards will be presented immediately after your speech. The audience consists of 150 people: parents, teachers, students, administrators, and some representatives from the community. Dinner was average. It is about 8:30 p.m. You have been asked to keep your speech to about ten minutes in length.

1. What is the specific purpose of your speech? (5 points)
2. Write, in as much detail as you feel is necessary, an outline of your speech. Use the proper format and include your thesis statement. (15 points)
3. Write out *exactly* the opening to your speech. Identify the type of introduction you selected. (15 points)
4. Write out *exactly* the conclusion of your speech. Identify which type of conclusion you selected. (15 points)
5. What process will you follow to practice your speech? (10 points)
6. What will you do to cope with any nervousness you may feel? (10 points)
7. Will you use any visual aids? Why/why not? (5 points)
8. What do you intend to include in your speech to hold the attention of your audience? (10 points)
9. Analyze your audience by answering the following questions:

(a) What do you *know* about the audience? (b) What can you *assume* about the audience? (c) What can you reasonably expect from the audience in terms of behavior? (15 points)

Final Exam

This exam is designed to determine whether or not you can apply the tools of Public Speaking to a particular speaking situation, to show that you understand the concepts involved. I suggest you read all of the questions before answering any of them.

SITUATION: You are just completing your first year of college. You have been invited to speak at the high school from which you graduated last year. The major purpose of this student assembly is to encourage the students to continue their education by attending college next year. Therefore, you have decided to give a persuasive speech. The audience is composed of high school juniors, seniors, teachers, and a few administrators (about 1,250 people). You are the third and last speaker. The first speaker was an administrator who spoke on "Why You Should Attend College." The two speeches were similar and the students are bored and very restless. It is 1:30 p.m. You have been asked to keep your speech about ten minutes in length.

The following questions all refer to *your* speech for this occasion. Remember, it is a persuasive speech.

1. Write out the proposition for your speech. (8 points)
2. As part of your research for your speech, you have decided to visit the local library. What sources will you consult? Why? (12 points)
3. As a student of public speaking, you know that the interview you are going to conduct also can provide excellent, usable material for your speech. How will you prepare for this interview? Explain the six different types of questions you might ask during the interview. What should be your behavior during the interview? (25 points)
4. What is credibility? How will you demonstrate credibility during your speech? (15 points)
5. Your text states "You are more likely to persuade an audience when you give them logical reasons for their support." On what basis will you determine which reasons and supporting evidence will best convince your audience? (20 points)
6. Which method of organization will you use? Why? (10 points)
7. When attempting to motivate an audience, your test refers to three basic strategies that can be used; cost-reward; cognitive dissonance; and basic needs. Which strategy(s) will you use? Why? (10 points)

I was very pleased with the results of the two exams. The students felt challenged as they had to do more than just memorize information from the text. I was able to help individual students more since their answers showed the areas in which they were weak and, at the same time, showed their strengths. I gave a lot of written and oral feedback to the class as a whole, and to specific individuals. Not only was the exam an effective method of evaluation; it also was a useful learning tool for the students.

Jeanette L. Wall

A Student-Devised Evaluation Form

Goal: To describe an in-class activity in which students devise an objective critique, for form evaluating the delivery aspects of graded speeches.

Speech-making involves material selection, organization, and delivery. The public speaking instructor can specify parameters for material selection and organization by defining the assignment (e.g., a 4-6 minute informative speech containing an introduction, body with 3 main points in which 2 sources are cited, and a conclusion). Further, students learn material on selection and organization skills in both the written and oral communication classrooms. However, the speech teacher has sole responsibility for instruction in delivery. Further, the speech assignment generally does not provide parameters for delivery. Indeed, it is difficult to identify objective criteria for evaluating delivery aspects of in-class speeches. Although 9 of the 13 evaluation forms recommended by D.G. Bock and E.H. Bock in their *Evaluating Classroom Speaking* (Annandale, VA: Speech Communication Association, 1981) contain delivery elements, they list nonspecific criteria, such as "Is the speaker communicative?" and "Were the gestures meaningful?" Such general criteria may lead to disagreement among multiple critiquers, as well as disagreement between speaker and the grade assigner.

This essay describes an in-class activity in which students devise an objective critique form for evaluating the delivery aspects of graded speeches. Because the students themselves devise the form, they do not complain about the instructor's selections of evaluation criteria. Further, they share consensual meaning regarding the specific criteria, thus eliminating most disagreements between multiple critiquers.

The activity requires 1-2 class periods and should be conducted before any graded speeches begin. The period begins with a "pop quiz." Students write answers to the following 3 oral questions:

1. Sam appeared nervous as he spoke. What did Sam do with his hands?
2. Susan gave an excellent speech! What was Susan's voice like?
3. During his speech, John maintained good eye contact. How often did he look at his notes?

Next, the instructor reviews the answers orally, noting the wide variety of answers. Then s/he explains that specific (vs. general and/or evaluative) feedback provides the speaker with more helpful information by offering descriptions of problematic, as well as positive, behaviors. At this point, the instructor talks briefly about behavior descriptions, defining the concept (a specific description of an observable behavior such as, "John looked at his notes during the first 30 seconds of his speech,") and noting the nonjudgmental nature of such descriptions.

Next, groups containing 3-4 students are formed to generate lists of behavior actions that describe excellent delivery in extemporaneous speech making. The teacher assigns each group an aspect of delivery, such as eye contact, gestures, body movement and posture, voice, use of props and visual aids, audience inand language, to discuss for the next 7-10 minutes. When the volvement, groups complete their task, one at a time, they write their lists of behavior descriptions on the chalkboard and the teacher facilitates class discussion of the lists. Behavior descriptions are added, deleted, and/or modified until each class member agrees that the list defines excellent delivery for that topic.

The class uses behavior descriptions as a check list which, after the teacher adds informational components and additional evaluation criteria (such as organization), becomes the critique forms used by the teacher and students to evaluate graded, in-class speeches. The following is an example of a critique form generated in this manner.

SPEAKER: ________
OBSERVER: ________
TOPIC ________
DATE: ________
TIME: ________

Eye Contact

______ Maintained eye contact during first 7 seconds
______ Had direct eye contact 80-85% of the time
______ Coverage of entire audience during speech
______ Used eye expression for emphasis
______ Ratio of 2:1 looking-at-audience to looking-at-notes

Gestures

______ Used hand gestures for emphasis
______ Gestured to regain attention of audience, if necessary
______ Size of gestures varied with size of audience
______ Facial expression appropriate to material

Body Movement and Posture

______ Used casual, relaxed stance 100% of the time
______ Moved away from lectern for visual variety
______ Had erect body posture 100% of the time
______ Changed body orientation to cover entire audience

Voice

______ Used steady, confident voice 100% of the time
______ Used clear, distinct pronunciation 100% of the time
______ Heard clearly in back of room 100% of the time
______ Used inflections (vs. monotone)
______ Used increased rate of speech with enthusiasm

Language

______ Defined words audience might not understand
______ Avoided racist, sexist, ageist language

Transition and Pauses

______ Smooth transitions that clearly divided main points
______ Paused to emphasize and divide points

Visual Aids/Props

______ Large enough to be seen clearly in back of room
______ Shown only when discussed
______ Looked at audience rather than visual aid
______ Set up visual aid before speech, if possible

Introduction

______ Used effective attention getting device
______ Emphasized clearly stated thesis
______ Previewed main points
______ Established credibility

Body

______ Used 3-5 main points
______ Stated and explained subpoints
______ Cited evidence

Conclusion

______ Restated thesis
______ Summarized main points
______ Established finality

Lynne Webb